WWW.SHOOT.CO.UK

@SHOOTMAGAZINE

Published 2014.

Pedigree Books Limited, Beech Hill House, Walnut
Gardens, Exeter, Devon EX4 4DH

www.pedigreebooks.com
shoot@pedigreegroup.co.uk

EDITOR **DANIEL TYLER**
ASSISTANT EDITOR: **JAMES BEAVIS**
DESIGN **JAMES BOWLER**

CONTENTS

KING CRISTIANO

MADRID AND PORTUGAL STAR IS ON TOP OF THE WORLD

Real Madrid superstar Cristiano Ronaldo will go down as one of the all time greats when he decides to hang up his boots.

The goalscoring machine collected his second Ballon d'Or – awarded to the best player on the planet – in 2014.

However, life wasn't always as easy or glamorous for the Portuguese superstar.

Born in Santo Antonio, a neighborhood of Funchal, Madeira, Ronaldo was named after then US President Ronald Reagan, who was his dad's favourite actor.

He lived in relative poverty as a child and was expelled from school at the age of 14 before deciding to focus on football.

A year later he was diagnosed with a racing heart, which threatened his football career before it had even kicked-off, but a successful operation saw the talented teenager back on the field in no time.

After excelling in the youth teams of Andorinha and Nacional, the awesome attacker was snapped up by Sporting Lisbon where he scored twice on his professional debut as a 17-year-old.

Following an impressive performance in a pre-season match against Manchester United, the then Red Devils manager Alex Ferguson took Ronaldo to Old Trafford for £12.24m.

Despite showing flashes of quality, the young star found it tough to adapt to English football in his first few seasons before springing to life in 2006 by scoring 23 goals as United won the Premier League for the first time in four years.

His next two campaigns brought a whole host of trophies and 68 goals before a world-record £80m transfer to Spanish giants Real Madrid in July 2009.

Unbelievably, the flying forward got even better after moving to Spain and netted his 250th goal for the La Liga giants in just his 243rd game.

King Cristiano has also been the main man for his country as well as Real Madrid in recent years.

The famous number 7 won his 100th international cap in 2012 and became Portugal's record scorer when he netted the first of two goals in a 5-1 win against Cameroon in March 2014.

Captaining his country at three of his six major tournament appearances and scoring all four goals in their 2014 World Cup play-off win against Sweden can also be added to the twice European Golden Shoe winner's endless list of achievements.

RONALDO ON...

COMPETITION

"Competition helps me to be a better player, of course. But not only competition with Messi. Also other players of a high level like those I see in the Premier League and in other leagues - Luis Suarez, Andres Iniesta, Neymar, Gareth Bale, Diego Costa or Radamel Falcao."

SIR ALEX FERGUSON

"Sir Alex Ferguson is my second dad - he helped me a lot to improve and Mr. Mourinho too because they are experienced managers who win many things, so for me they are the best coaches."

MANCHESTER UNITED

"I have good memories from Manchester and when I watch sometimes the games I miss it a lot because it's a part of me I left in England."

REAL MADRID

"Real Madrid is now my home. I hope that I'm here until I retire. This is a great club. My only goal is to be here and to play at this club until, maybe, the end of my career. I just want to win trophies."

REPRESENTING PORTUGAL

"It was on August 20th, 2003, against Kazakhstan, that I put on our national shirt for the first time. It was one of the most memorable moments of my life and a path which I am proud of. I would like to thank all of those who helped me reach over 100 caps."

WHAT THEY SAY

"He is always there scoring goals in all the games and taking part in his club and national side. He has been doing that for many years and whether he is at his peak or a bit below it makes no difference."
Lionel Messi. Barcelona and Argentina star.

"I knew he would improve, but I did not expect him to score the goals he has scored. It is phenomenal. He has flourished in Madrid. He has fitness, speed, he is never injured, plays every week... that is unique in the modern day game. He never asks for a rest, wants to play all the time, these are exceptional qualities."
Sir Alex Ferguson, Ex-Manchester United boss.

"Cristiano is living proof that no matter how much talent you have as a youngster, you have to work hard in order to be successful. Thousands of hours of graft both in the gym and on the training ground turned him into the perfect specimen. I'm still truly astonished by his drive and determination to stay at the top,"
Rio Ferdinand, ex-Manchester United team-mate.

"Coaching him was the highlight of my career. He's the most professional player I've ever met."
Jose Mourinho, current Chelsea and ex-Real Madrid manager.

FACT FILE

Cristiano Ronaldo
Position: Forward
Birth date: February 5, 1985
Birth place: Funchal, Madeira, Portugal
Height: 1.85m (6ft 1in)
Clubs: Sporting Lisbon, Manchester United, Real Madrid
International: Portugal
Twitter: @Cristiano

GOALS PER SEASON

Sporting Lisbon
2002-03 Games: 31 Goals: 5
Manchester United
2003-04 Games: 40 Goals: 6
2004-05 Games: 50 Goals: 9
2005-06 Games: 47 Goals: 12
2006-07 Games: 53 Goals: 23
2007-08 Games: 49 Goals: 42
2008-09 Games: 53 Goals: 26
Real Madrid
2009-10 Games: 35 Goals: 33
2010-11 Games: 54 Goals: 53
2011-12 Games: 55 Goals: 60
2012-13 Games: 55 Goals: 55
2013-14 Games: 47 Goals: 51

Total: Games: 569 Goals: 375

HONOURS

Manchester United
Premier League: 2007, 2008, 2009
FA Cup: 2004
League Cup: 2006, 2009
Champions League: 2008
Club World Cup: 2008
Community Shield: 2007

Real Madrid
La Liga: 2012
Copa del Rey: 2011, 2014
Supercopa de Espana: 2012

MILESTONES

October 2002: Sporting Lisbon professional debut and first senior goal
August 2003: Made a £12.24m transfer to Manchester United
Manchester United debut
International debut
November 2003: First Manchester United goal
May 2004: FA Cup winner
July 2004: Euro 2004 runner-up
February 2006: League Cup winner
June 2006: Played for Portugal at World Cup 2006
April 2007: Named PFA Player, Young Player and Football Writers' Association Footballer of the Year.
May 2007: 50th United goal
Premier League champion
October 2007: 50th international cap
May 2008: Premier League champion
Champions League final winner
June 2008: Played for Portugal at Euro 2008
November 2008: 100th United goal
December 2008: Club World Cup winner
January 2009: Ballon d'Or winner
March 2009: League Cup winner
May 2009: Premier League champion
Champions League runner-up
July 2009: World record £80m transfer to Real Madrid
August 2009: Real Madrid debut and first Real Madrid goal
June 2010: Captained Portugal at World Cup 2010
November 2010: 50th Madrid goal
April 2011: Copa del Rey champion
October 2011: 100th Madrid goal
May 2012: La Liga champion
June 2012: Captained Portugal at Euro 2012
August 2012: Supercopa de Espana winner
September 2012: 150th Madrid goal
October 2012: 100th international cap
May 2013: 200th Madrid goal
January 2014: Ballon d'Or winner
March 2014: Portugal's record goalscorer
April 2014: Copa del Rey champion
May 2014: 250th Madrid goal
June 2014: Captained Portugal at World Cup 2014

YOUNG · GUNS

PAUL POGBA

D.O.B: 15.3.1993

CENTRAL MIDFIELDER

INTERNATIONAL:
FRANCE

BIRTH PLACE:
LAGNY-SUR-MARNE, FRANCE

The all-action midfielder was in Manchester United's academy from 2009-2011 before he made the step up to the first-team in the 2011-12 season. However, he made only a handful of appearances and turned down a new contract at Old Trafford before moving to Italy to play for Juventus in Serie A. Known for his power, skill and eye for goal, Pogba has already become a key player for the Italian giants and the France national team. This is a boy destined to stay at the top for a long time to come.

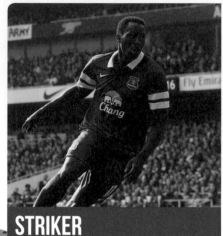

ROMELU LUKAKU

D.O.B: 13.5.1993

STRIKER

INTERNATIONAL:
BELGIUM

BIRTH PLACE:
ANTWERP, BELGIUM

With his stature and how long he has been around, it is easy to forget that the Belgium international is still a youngster in footballing terms. A hugely successful spell in his home country with Anderlecht led to a move to Chelsea, and since then he has impressed in loan spells at West Brom and Everton in the Premier League, as he looks to make the grade at Stamford Bridge. Known for his power, pace and lethal shot, it is hard to ignore the comparisons with Blues legend Didier Drogba.

ADNAN JANUZAJ

D.O.B: 5.2.1995

WINGER

INTERNATIONAL:
BELGIUM

BIRTH PLACE:
BRUSSELS, BELGIUM

In a poor 2013-14 season for Manchester United, the young winger was one of the club's few shining lights. The Belgium international moved to Old Trafford at the age of 16 from Anderlecht and made an impression on David Moyes at the start of the 2013-14 season. After starting some matches, Januzaj soon caught the eye with his ability on the ball, pace to get past defenders and accurate shooting. This is a player that we will be hearing a lot more about in the coming years.

KURT ZOUMA

D.O.B: 27.9.1994

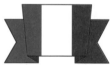

CENTRE BACK

INTERNATIONAL:
FRANCE U-21

BIRTH PLACE:
LYON, FRANCE

Signed by Chelsea for £12m at the end of 2014 January transfer window from French side Saint-Etienne, Zouma is one of the top prospects in world football. The centre-half made his debut for the Ligue 1 outfit at the age of 16 and has gone on to impress, so much so that Jose Mourinho decided to take him to Stamford Bridge. His career has been slightly disrupted by injury but he has already shown that he has the leadership, power and technique to make it at the highest level.

WE ALL LOVE WATCHING PLAYERS LIKE CRISTIANO RONALDO, LIONEL MESSI AND NEYMAR, BUT A NEW BREED OF YOUNGSTERS ARE CONSTANTLY COMING THROUGH HOPING TO FOLLOW IN THE FOOTSTEPS OF THOSE SUPERSTARS. HERE *SHOOT* IDENTIFIES A CROP OF TALENTED STARLETS TO WATCH ACROSS THE WORLD FOOTBALL...

ALEN HALILOVIC

D.O.B: 18.6.1996

INTERNATIONAL: CROATIA

ATTACKING MIDFIELDER

BIRTH PLACE:
DUBROVNIK, CROATIA

Dubbed the next Lionel Messi, this young midfielder has already made such an impact in football that he has become the youngest goalscorer in the Croatian league for Dinamo Zagreb, the youngest debutant for his national side, and secured a move to Barcelona on a five-year deal. He is set to start his career with the Spanish giants in their B team, but it wouldn't be a surprise to see him break into Luis Enrique's first-team plans in the near future.

DIEGO POYET

D.O.B: 8.4.1995

INTERNATIONAL: ENGLAND U-17

CENTRAL MIDFIELDER

BIRTH PLACE:
ZARAGOZA, SPAIN

The son of Sunderland manager and former Uruguay star Gus Poyet, Diego is showing that a talent for football certainly runs in the family. Despite only breaking into the Charlton Athletic first-team in January 2014, the former England youth international won the club's Player of the Season award after a number of impressive displays in the middle of the pitch. A midfielder with an eye for a pass, Poyet is happy to do both sides of the game and has a mature head on young shoulders.

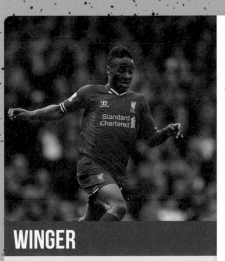

RAHEEM STERLING

D.O.B: 8.12.1994

INTERNATIONAL: ENGLAND

WINGER

BIRTH PLACE:
KINGSTON, JAMAICA

Before the 2013-14 season, there were doubts as to whether Sterling was going to have the impact that had been predicted when he burst onto the scene in 2012. However, he soon became an instrumental figure in Liverpool's chase for the Premier League title, so much so that he has become a key figure for both club and country. Known for his pace, trickery and ability with the ball, the youngster has found the end product that is so often missing from speedy wingers.

LUKE SHAW

D.O.B: 12.7.1995

INTERNATIONAL: ENGLAND

LEFT-BACK

BIRTH PLACE:
KINGSTON UPON THAMES, ENGLAND

By the end of the 2013-14 season, aged just 18, Shaw had already made more than 50 appearances for Southampton in the Premier League. Widely regarded as one of the best youngsters in Europe, his form saw him receive his first cap for England and he was also named in the 23-man squad for the World Cup in Brazil. Known for his marauding attacking runs, the full-back looks set for a long career at the very top level. Sealed a £27m move to Manchester United in June 2014.

PREMIER LEAGUE

The 2013-14 Premier League season will be remembered for one of change. Manchester United, the reigning champions, began life without the greatest manager of all time Sir Alex Ferguson, and former Everton boss David Moyes was tasked with defending the Red Devils' title.

However, it was to be a disastrous season for United as they finished seventh, their lowest position since the division was formed in 1992. This, along with no Champions League football next season for the first time since 1995-96 resulted in Moyes losing his job after just 10 months, with United legend Ryan Giggs put in charge until the end of the season.

The title race was contested by big spending Manchester City, surprise package Liverpool and Chelsea. The Merseyside club were hoping to secure their first ever Premier League crown, and went on an impressive run which saw them win 11 league matches in a row. But they slipped up against Chelsea, losing 2-0 at Anfield and Crystal Palace; where they threw away a 3-0 lead to draw 3-3, allowing City to secure their second top flight trophy in three seasons.

The title went down to the final day of the season, but there was to be no last minute drama like there was in 2012 with Sergio Aguero, as Manuel Pellegrini's side comfortably beat West Ham United 2-0 at the Etihad thanks to goals from Samir Nasri and captain Vincent Kompany.

Liverpool fell just short of the title, but secured Champions League football for the first time in four years, along with Jose Mourinho's Chelsea and Arsenal, who secured qualification under Arsene Wenger for the 17th season in a row.

Newly promoted Crystal Palace and Hull City both enjoyed successful seasons. The Eagles were five points off safety before manager Tony Pulis replaced Ian Holloway, but the Welshman guided the South London side to a remarkable 11th placed finish. Hull finished in 16th place, but did reach the first FA Cup final in their history.

Cardiff City didn't enjoy the same success as their other fellow promoted sides. The Bluebirds finished rock bottom after a turbulent season which saw manager Malky Mackay sacked in December and replaced by Manchester United legend Ole Gunnar Solskjaer.

Fulham, who had been in the top flight since 2001, and Norwich City will also play Championship football in the 2014-15 season.

NEW CLUBS 2014-15

BURNLEY

LEICESTER CITY

QUEENS PARK RANGERS

THE GREAT ESCAPE

Sunderland produced the miracle of the season after staying up against all odds. The Black Cats looked doomed for the drop as they sat seven points adrift of safety with six games remaining. But Uruguayan boss Gus Poyet helped produce the miracle he said they needed to survive by collecting 13 points from a possible 18. Wins at Chelsea and Manchester United plus a draw at Manchester City amazingly saw them keep their heads above water.

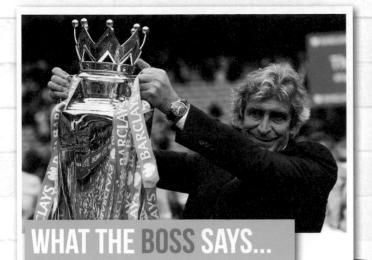

WHAT THE BOSS SAYS...

"We were the best team in the Premier League. It was a very special season for us, we were hardly never top, we had games postponed. But the players believed in me. It's a very special group.
The players always believed what I told them. To play the way I like, because that is what football must be like in a great team. I think this team cannot be satisfied with just one title" – **Manuel Pellegrini**

WHAT THE PLAYERS SAID...

"It's a great achievement. It will be recognised. We're building a big club and I'm proud to be part of this. We did everything right this season. We've had a busy schedule and we've come through. As the fans say, we fight to the end."
Vincent Kompany, Manchester City captian.

"We have to congratulate Manchester City. They been the best over 38 games so congratulations to them."
Steven Gerrard, Liverpool captain.

"I feel amazing. It's been a hard season and we've come out the other end the best way possible. This has been a hard slog but we've beaten some great teams and we're really proud with what we've achieved. This is football at its best - I love the game and I love this club."
Joe Hart, Manchester City goalkeeper.

STATS

TOP SCORER: LUIS SUAREZ (LIVERPOOL) - 31
MOST ASSISTS: STEVEN GERRARD (LIVERPOOL) - 14
CLEAN SHEETS (CLUB): CHELSEA - 19
CLEAN SHEETS (PLAYER): PETR CECH (CHELSEA) - 16
MOST GOALS: MANCHESTER CITY - 102
MOST GOALS AGAINST: FULHAM - 85
MOST GOALS IN A GAME: MANCHESTER CITY 6-3 ARSENAL, CARDIFF CITY 3-6 LIVERPOOL
BIGGEST WIN: MANCHESTER CITY 7-0 NORWICH CITY
BIGGEST CROWD: MANCHESTER UNITED 4-1 ASTON VILLA - 75,368
MOST YELLOWS: ASTON VILLA - 78
MOST REDS: SUNDERLAND - 7

2013-2014 PREMIER LEAGUE TABLE

		PL	GD	PTS
1	MANCHESTER CITY	38	65	86
2	LIVERPOOL	38	51	84
3	CHELSEA	38	44	82
4	ARSENAL	38	27	79
5	EVERTON	38	22	72
6	TOTTENHAM HOTSPUR	38	4	69
7	MANCHESTER UNITED	38	21	64
8	SOUTHAMPTON	38	8	56
9	STOKE CITY	38	-7	50
10	NEWCASTLE UNITED	38	-16	49
11	CRYSTAL PALACE	38	-15	45
12	SWANSEA CITY	38	0	42
13	WEST HAM UNITED	38	-11	40
14	SUNDERLAND	38	-19	38
15	ASTON VILLA	38	-22	38
16	HULL CITY	38	-15	37
17	WEST BROMWICH ALBION	38	-16	36
18	NORWICH CITY	38	-34	33
19	FULHAM	38	-45	32
20	CARDIFF CITY	38	-42	30

ALL TIME TOP FLIGHT

PREMIER LEAGUE

STATS, FACTS & TRIVIA YOU NEED TO KNOW!

Fewest defeats:
Arsenal (2003–04)
0

Most consecutive wins:
Arsenal — 14
(February 10, 2002 –
August 24, 2002)

Biggest undefeated streak:
Arsenal — 49 games
(May 7, 2003 –
October 24, 2004)

Youngest player:
16 Years 65 Days
Matthew Briggs
(Fulham)

Oldest player:
43 Years 162 Days
John Burridge
(Manchester City)

Most points in a season:
Chelsea (2004–05) — 95

Fewest points:
Derby County (2007–08) — 11

Most goals in a season (player):
Andrew Cole (Newcastle United, 1993–94), Alan Shearer (Blackburn Rovers, 1994–95) –34

Most goals in a season (club):
Chelsea (2009–10) — 103

Fewest goals:
Derby County (2007–08) — 20

Most relegations:
Crystal Palace - 4

Fewest wins in a season: Derby County (2007–08) **1**

Most defeats: Ipswich Town (1994–95), Sunderland (2005–06), Derby County (2007–08) **29**

Most appearances:
Ryan Giggs
(Manchester United)
632

TOP SCORER:

Top scorer: Alan Shearer
(Blackburn Rovers and
Newcastle United)

260

Most wins: Chelsea

29

(2004-05, 2005-06)

MOST ASSISTS:

Ryan Giggs (Manchester United)

131

**Most titles:
Manchester United**

13

Biggest crowd: Manchester United 4-1 Blackburn Rovers (March 31, 2007) — 76,098

Biggest win: Manchester United 9-0 Ipswich Town (March 4, 1995)

Most goals in a game: Portsmouth 7-4 Reading (September 29, 2007)

Longest managerial tenure: Sir Alex Ferguson (Manchester United) — 6452 days

Shortest Managerial tenure : Les Reed (Charlton Athletic) — 41 days

MOST YELLOW CARDS:

Lee Bowyer (Leeds United,
Newcastle United, West Ham
United, Birmingham City)

Paul Scholes
(Manchester United)

Kevin Davies
(Southampton,
Blackburn Rovers,
Bolton Wanderers)

MOST RED CARDS:

Richard Dunne (Everton,
Manchester City and
Aston Villa)

Patrick Vieira
(Arsenal)

Duncan Ferguson
(Everton and Newcastle United)

CHAMPIONSHIP

LEICESTER CITY WON PROMOTION BACK TO THE PREMIER LEAGUE FOR THE FIRST TIME IN A DECADE.

The Foxes won 31 of their 46 games, which saw them collect a whopping 102 points. They clinched promotion after beating Sheffield Wednesday 2-1, and wrapped up the Championship title in April after defeating Bolton Wanderers 1-0 at the Reebok Stadium, finishing nine points clear of second-placed Burnley.

The Clarets had a remarkable season, with manager Sean Dyche leading the club back to the Premier League where they enjoyed just one season in 2009-10. The Turf Moor outfit, who were one of the favourites for relegation before the campaign kicked off, saw strikers Danny Ings and Sam Vokes net a total of 41 goals.

As for the bottom of the table, Yeovil were relegated after just one season in the Championship. The Somerset club, who had the smallest budget in the league, found life in the second tier too much, and their fate was sealed after a 2-0 defeat at Brighton and Hove Albion in April.

Barnsley will also be playing their football in League One after falling through the trap door. The Yorkshire side had stayed up on the last day the previous season, but their 3-1 loss at Middlesbrough meant they couldn't repeat their escape. Yorkshire rivals Doncaster Rovers will be joining Barnsley in the third tier after a dramatic final day. Rovers were safe until an injury time goal from Birmingham City's Paul Caddis kept the Blues up and sent Donny straight back down.

PLAY-OFFS

Derby County thrashed Brighton & Hove Albion 6-2 on aggregate, while QPR edged Wigan Athletic 2-1 to set-up a play-off final between the Rams and the R's at Wembley Stadium.

And it was the London side that went straight back to the Premier League after a 1-0 win.

A 90th minute goal from substitute Bobby Zamora secured promotion for the Hoops, who were largely outplayed by Steve McClaren's side.

It looked even more unlikely when boss Harry Redknapp saw midfielder Gary O'Neil sent off, but Zamora's side-footed finish was enough to snatch victory.

STATS

TOP SCORER: ROSS MCCORMACK (LEEDS UNITED) - 28

MOST ASSISTS: CRAIG CONWAY (BLACKBURN ROVERS) - 14

CLEAN SHEETS (CLUB): BRIGHTON - 20

CLEAN SHEETS (PLAYER): TOM HEATON (BURNLEY) - 19

MOST GOALS: DERBY COUNTY - 84

MOST GOALS AGAINST: BARNSLEY - 77

MOST GOALS IN A GAME: DERBY COUNTY 4-4 IPSWICH TOWN, LEICESTER CITY 5-3 BOLTON WANDERERS, READING 7-1 BOLTON WANDERERS

BIGGEST WIN: READING 7-1 BOLTON WANDERERS, SHEFFIELD WEDNESDAY 6-0 LEEDS UNITED

BIGGEST CROWD: DERBY COUNTY 5-0 NOTTINGHAM FOREST - 33,004

MOST YELLOWS: WATFORD - 99

MOST REDS: BLACKPOOL - 10

WHAT THE BOSS SAYS...

"I am delighted for everyone associated with the club. It has been a long time coming. I am really looking forward to seeing a lot of our players performing in the top flight because I think they will do very well."

Nigel Pearson, Leicester boss.

NEW CLUBS 2014-15

 WOLVES

 ROTHERHAM UNITED

 BRENTFORD

 CARDIFF CITY

 FULHAM

 NORWICH CITY

2013-2014 CHAMPIONSHIP TABLE

		PL	GD	PTS
1	LEICESTER	46	+40	102
2	BURNLEY	46	+35	93
3	DERBY	46	+32	85
4	QPR	46	+16	80
5	WIGAN ATH	46	+13	73
6	BRIGHTON	46	+15	72
7	READING	46	+14	71
8	BLACKBURN	46	+8	70
9	IPSWICH TOWN	46	+6	68
10	BOURNEMTH	46	+1	66
11	NOTTM FOR	46	+3	65
12	MIDDLESBRO	46	+12	64
13	WATFORD	46	+10	60
14	BOLTON	46	-1	59
15	LEEDS UTD	46	-8	57
16	SHEFF WED	46	-2	53
17	HUDDERSFLD	46	-7	53
18	CHARLTON	46	-20	51
19	MILLWALL	46	-28	48
20	BLACKPOOL	46	-28	46
21	BIRMINGHAM	46	-16	44
22	DONCASTER	46	-31	44
23	BARNSLEY	46	-33	39
24	YEOVIL TOWN	46	-31	37

LEAGUE 1

WOLVERHAMPTON WANDERERS WERE PROMOTED BACK TO THE CHAMPIONSHIP AT THE FIRST TIME OF ASKING AFTER A RECORD-BREAKING SEASON.

Kenny Jackett's side broke the record points total for the third division, collecting 103 in all. They also equalled the league's clean sheet record with Wanderers failing to concede on 25 occasions throughout the campaign. The Molineux outfit, who had suffered back-to-back relegations the previous two terms, sealed promotion in April with a 2-0 win over Crewe Alexandra.

Brentford will be joining Wolves in the second tier for the first time in 21 years after claiming second spot. The Bees beat Preston North End 1-0 to erase the heartache of 12 months ago which saw them dramatically miss out on automatic promotion on the final day to Doncaster Rovers.

At the other end, Stevenage's three-year stay in League One ended after they were relegated. Graham Westley's side, who finished eight points from safety, officially dropped to the fourth tier after a 3-1 defeat to Bristol City.

Shrewsbury were also relegated after two seasons in League One, while Carlisle United and Tranmere Rovers, who finished just outside the play-offs in 2012-13 and had spent 13 seasons in the third tier, also suffered the dreaded drop.

PLAY-OFFS

Fourth placed Rotherham United saw off Preston North End 4-2 on aggregate, while Leyton Orient snuck past play-off specialists Peterborough United 3-2.

At Wembley, it was United who secured back-to-back promotions after defeating the O's in a penalty shoot-out.

Russell Slade's side led 2-0 at half time thanks to goals from Moses Odubajo and Dean Cox, but an Alex Revell brace, including a stunning 30-yard half volley, levelled the score before Steve Evans' side triumphed 4-3 on penalties.

STATS

TOP SCORER: SAM BALDOCK (BRISTOL CITY), BRITT ASSOMBALONGA (PETERBOROUGH UNITED) - 28

MOST ASSISTS: BAKARY SAKO (WOLVERHAMPTON WANDERERS) - 14

CLEAN SHEETS (CLUB):
WOLVERHAMPTON WANDERERS - 25

CLEAN SHEETS (PLAYER): CARL IKEME (WOLVERHAMPTON WANDERERS) - 22

MOST GOALS:
WOLVERHAMPTON WANDERERS - 89

MOST GOALS AGAINST:
CREWE ALEXANDRA - 80

MOST GOALS IN A GAME: WOLVERHAMPTON WANDERERS 6-4 ROTHERHAM UNITED

BIGGEST WIN: ROTHERHAM UNITED 6-0 NOTTS COUNTY

BIGGEST CROWD: WOLVERHAMPTON WANDERERS 6-4 ROTHERHAM UNITED - 30,110

MOST YELLOWS: NOTTS COUNTY - 88

MOST REDS: PETERBOROUGH UNITED, TRANMERE ROVERS - 8

WHAT THE BOSS SAYS...

"You need to set short-term goals and this has been the first step in our overall plan. Our aim when we come back in the summer is to get back to the Premier League. My staff and players, we are here to get promoted next season."
Kenny Jackett, Wolves boss.

NEW CLUBS 2014-15

CHESTERFIELD

 BARNSLEY

SCUNTHORPE UNITED

FLEETWOOD TOWN

ROCHDALE

 DONCASTER

YEOVIL TOWN

2013-2014 LEAGUE 1 TABLE

		PL	GD	PTS
1	WOLVES	46	58	103
2	BRENTFORD	46	29	94
3	LEYTON ORIENT	46	40	86
4	ROTHERHAM	46	28	86
5	PRESTON	46	26	85
6	PETERBOROUGH	46	14	74
7	SHEFF UTD	46	2	67
8	SWINDON	46	4	66
9	PORT VALE	46	-14	61
10	MK DONS	46	-2	60
11	BRADFORD	46	3	59
12	BRISTOL CITY	46	3	58
13	WALSALL	46	0	58
14	CRAWLEY	46	-6	57
15	OLDHAM	46	-9	56
16	COLCHESTER	46	-8	53
17	GILLINGHAM	46	-19	53
18	COVENTRY	46	-3	51
19	CREWE	46	-26	51
20	NOTTS COUNTY	46	-13	50
21	TRANMERE	46	-27	47
22	CARLISLE	46	-33	45
23	SHREWSBURY	46	-21	42
24	STEVENAGE	46	-26	42

LEAGUE 2

CHESTERFIELD WERE PROMOTED BACK TO LEAGUE ONE JUST TWO SEASONS AFTER BEING RELEGATED FROM THE THIRD TIER AS BOSS PAUL COOK GUIDED THE CLUB TO THE LEAGUE TWO TITLE.

It was a tight battle for promotion, but The Spireites secured promotion with a 2-0 victory at Burton Albion thanks to two goals from Jay O'Shea.

The title race went down to the last day of the season, but the Proact Stadium outfit finished three points clear of Scunthorpe United and Rochdale as they clinched the championship with a 2-1 win over fourth placed Fleetwood Town. Scunthorpe went on a record-breaking run as they managed to go 28 games without defeat - enough to ensure an immediate return to the third tier. Striker Sam Winnall finished as the division's top scorer

with an impressive 23 goals. In third, Keith Hill's Rochdale clinched the final automatic promotion spot, returning to League One after a two-year absence.

At the bottom, Torquay United were relegated to the Conference for the first time in five seasons after suffering 25 defeats from their 46 games.

The Gulls were surprisingly joined by Bristol Rovers, who were relegated from the Football League for the first time in 94 years after losing at home to Mansfield Town on the last day.

The Pirates went down at the expense of Wycombe Wanderers, who survived thanks to a 3-0 win at already relegated Torquay.

PLAY-OFFS

Fleetwood Town and Burton Albion secured a spot in the play-off final after seeing off York City and Southend United respectively in the semi-finals.

And it was the Cod Army who were promoted to League One for the first time in the club's history, after defeating Burton Albion 1-0 at Wembley.

Antoni Sarcevic's free-kick with 15 minutes to go gave Fleetwood their sixth promotion in nine years and condemned The Brewers to more play-off heartache after Gary Rowett's side tasted a narrow defeat to Bradford City in the 2013 semi-finals.

WHAT THE BOSS SAYS...

"I'm delighted for the chairman and the board of directors and I'm delighted for the players. I'm so proud to be managing this club. We've had a few bumps and bruises along the way and we've had to take a bit of criticism but I've always felt this squad was comfortably good enough to be promoted and it's all been justified." *Paul Cook, Chesterfield boss*.

STATS

TOP SCORER: SAM WINNALL (SCUNTHORPE UNITED) - 23

MOST ASSISTS: KEVAN HURST (SOUTHEND UNITED) - 13

CLEAN SHEETS (CLUB): YORK CITY - 22

CLEAN SHEETS (PLAYER): SAM SLOCOMBE (SCUNTHORPE UNITED) - 21

MOST GOALS: CHESTERFIELD - 71

MOST GOALS AGAINST: PORTSMOUTH, TORQUAY UNITED - 66

MOST GOALS IN A GAME: FLEETWOOD TOWN 5-4 MANSFIELD TOWN

BIGGEST WIN: PLYMOUTH ARGYLE 5-0 MORECAMBE

BIGGEST CROWD: PORTSMOUTH 1-4 OXFORD UNITED - 18,181

MOST YELLOWS: MANSFIELD - 86

MOST REDS: ROCHDALE, WYCOMBE WANDERERS - 9

NEW CLUBS 2014-15

STEVENAGE

SHREWSBURY

TRANMERE

CARLISLE

LUTON TOWN

CAMBRIDGE

2013-2014 LEAGUE 2 TABLE

		PL	GD	PTS
1	CHESTERFIELD	46	31	84
2	SCUNTHORPE	46	24	81
3	ROCHDALE	46	21	81
4	FLEETWOOD	46	14	76
5	SOUTHEND	46	17	72
6	BURTON	46	5	72
7	YORK	46	11	71
8	OXFORD UTD	46	3	62
9	DAG & RED	46	-6	60
10	PLYMOUTH	46	-7	60
11	MANSFIELD	46	-9	60
12	BURY	46	8	59
13	PORTSMOUTH	46	-10	59
14	NEWPORT	46	-3	58
15	ACCRINGTON	46	-2	57
16	EXETER	46	-3	55
17	CHELTENHAM	46	-10	55
18	MORECAMBE	46	-12	54
19	HARTLEPOOL	46	-6	53
20	WIMBLEDON	46	-8	53
21	NORTHAMPTON	46	-15	53
22	WYCOMBE	46	-8	50
23	BRISTOL ROVERS	46	-11	50
24	TORQUAY	46	-24	45

ALL THE WINNERS!

WHO WON WHAT IN 2013-14

ENGLAND

FA CUP

ARSENAL

RUNNERS-UP: HULL CITY

Top Scorer: Britt Assombalonga (Peterborough United), Sam Clucas (Mansfield Town), Joe Garner (Preston North End) - **5**

Arsenal ended their nine-year wait for a trophy as they defeated Hull City 3-2 in a thrilling FA Cup final. The Gunners looked to be heading for heartbreak again when James Chester and Curtis Davies put the Tigers 2-0 up with just eight minuets played. But Arsene Wenger's side struck back through Santi Cazorla and Laurent Koscielny before Aaron Ramsey scored an extra-time winner.

LEAGUE CUP

MANCHESTER CITY

RUNNERS-UP: SUNDERLAND

Alvaro Negredo (Manchester City) - 5

Second half goals from Yaya Toure, Samir Nasri and Jesus Navas secured Manuel Pellegrini his first trophy in Europe. Sunderland had taken a shock first half lead through Fabio Borini but City proved too strong in the end.

COMMUNITY SHIELD

MANCHESTER UNITED

RUNNERS-UP: WIGAN ATHLETIC

Two goals from Robin van Persie saw the Red Devils ease to a 2-0 win against Championship side Wigan Athletic to hand David Moyes a winning start as manager.

JOHNSTONE'S PAINT TROPHY

PETERBOROUGH UNITED

RUNNERS-UP: CHESTERFIELD

Top Scorer: Danny Phillishirk
(Oldham Athletic) - **6**

Darren Ferguson's Peterborough United defeated League Two Chesterfield 3-1 at Wembley despite having a man sent off. Goals from Josh McQuoid, Shaun Brisley and Britt Assombalonga (pen) grabbed Posh their first major piece of silverware.

FA VASE

SHOLING

RUNNERS-UP: WEST AUCKLAND TOWN

Marvin Mclean's deflected strike 19 minutes from time secured Wessex Premier champions Sholing a 1-0 victory over West Auckland Town.

EUROPE

CHAMPIONS LEAGUE

REAL MADRID

**RUNNERS-UP:
ATLETICO MADRID**

Top Scorer: Cristiano Ronaldo
(Real Madrid) - **17**

Real Madrid won their tenth European Cup as they came from behind to beat city rivals Atletico 4-1 in Lisbon. Diego Godin's header looked to have secured Diego Simeone's side their first ever European Cup, but Sergio Ramos' 92nd minute equaliser took the game into extra time. Carlo Ancelotti's men found an extra gear against their tiring opponents and goals from Gareth Bale, Marcelo and a Cristiano Ronaldo penalty saw the Spanish giants clinch the trophy they'd so desperately craved for the first time since 2002.

FA TROPHY

CAMBRIDGE UNITED

RUNNERS-UP: GOSPORT BOROUGH

Cambridge United cruised to a 4-0 win over Conference South side Gosport Borough at Wembley. Goals from Ryan Bird, Luke Berry and a Ryan Donaldson brace eased the U's to their first FA Trophy triumph.

CONFERENCE

LUTON TOWN

RUNNERS-UP: CAMBRIDGE UNITED

The Hatters returned to the Football League for the first time in five years after losing just five of their 46 games and collecting 101 points. Runners-up Cambridge United defeated Gateshead 2-1 at Wembley to seal promotion via the play-offs.

EUROPA LEAGUE

SEVILLA

RUNNERS-UP: BENFICA

Top Scorer: Jonatan Soriano (FC Red Bull Salzburg) - **8**

Sevilla won their third European trophy in nine seasons by defeating Benfica 4-2 on penalties after a goalless draw in Turin. The Spanish side's goalkeeper Beto saved from Rodrigo and Oscar Cardoza to allow Kevin Gameiro to strike the winning spot kick. The defeat means the Portuguese giants have lost their last eight European finals.

EUROPEAN SUPER CUP

BAYERN MUNICH

RUNNERS-UP:
CHELSEA

Bayern Munich defeated 10-man Chelsea on penalties after an exciting 2-2 draw in Prague. Fernando Torres put the Blues ahead before Franck Ribery equalised. Eden Hazard then struck what looked like being the winner for the west London side, who had Ramires sent off, but Javi Martinez levelled matters with the last kick of the game. Romelu Lukaku missed the decisive spot kick. The Belgian's low shot was kept out by Manuel Neuer as the Germans triumphed 5-4.

WINNERS
UEFA SUPER CUP 2013

SCOTLAND

SCOTTISH PREMIER LEAGUE

CELTIC

RUNNERS-UP:
MOTHERWELL

Top scorer: Kris Commons (Celtic) - **23**

The Hoops secured their third title in a row as they finished on 99 points, 29 clear of runners-up Motherwell. The Bhoys were defeated just once in what was to be Neil Lennon's final term in charge.

SCOTTISH CUP

ST JOHNSTONE

RUNNERS-UP:
DUNDEE UNITED

St Johnstone won their first major trophy after defeating Dundee United 2-0 at Celtic Park. Goals either side of half time by Steven Anderson and Steven MacLean secured a historic victory for The Saints.

SCOTTISH LEAGUE CUP

ABERDEEN

RUNNERS-UP:
INVERNESS CALEDONIAN THISTLE

Aberdeen collected their first trophy since 1990 after beating Inverness Caledonian Thistle 4-2 on penalties. A goalless 120 minutes took the match to spot kicks where Adam Rooney struck the decisive blow after Billy McKay and Greg Tansey had missed for Caley.

UK & IRELAND

WELSH PREMIER LEAGUE	NIFL PREMIERSHIP	LEAGUE OF IRELAND (2013)
THE NEW SAINTS	**CLIFTONVILLE**	**ST PATRICK'S**
RUNNERS-UP: AIRBUS UK BROUGHTON	RUNNERS-UP: LINFIELD	RUNNERS-UP: DUNDALK
Top scorer: Chris Venables (Aberystwyth Town) - **24**	Top scorer: Joe Gormley (Cliftonville) - **27**	Top scorer: David O'Sullivan (Longford Town) - **21**

INDIVIDUAL

BALLON D'OR

CRISTIANO RONALDO

The Portugal star saw off competition from Lionel Messi and Franck Ribery to be voted the world's best player for the second time in his career. The forward had a fantastic 2013 for club and country, scoring 66 goals in 56 games.

PFA PLAYER & FOOTBALL WRITERS' FOOTBALLER OF THE YEAR

LUIS SUAREZ

The Liverpool striker put last year's disciplinary problems behind him as he helped the Reds finish second in the Premier League. The Uruguay star netted an incredible 31 league goals in just 33 appearances.

PFA YOUNG PLAYER OF THE YEAR

EDEN HAZARD

The Chelsea wing wizard had a fantastic season on the flank, scoring 14 goals in 34 Premier League games, including his first hat-trick for the Blues against Newcastle United.

LMA MANAGER OF THE SEASON

BRENDAN RODGERS

The Northern Irishman guided Liverpool to a second placed finish in the Premier League, just two points behind champions Manchester City in a season which saw them score a whopping 101 goals.

EUROPEAN GOLDEN SHOE

LUIS SUAREZ & CRISTIANO RONALDO

The Liverpool and Real Madrid superstars both scored 31 league goals as they had to make do with sharing the prize handed to Europe's most clinical player.

REST OF THE WORLD
2013-14

LA LIGA (SPAIN)

ATLETICO MADRID

SERIE A (ITALY)

JUVENTUS

LIGUE 1 (FRANCE)

PSG

BUNDESLIGA (GERMANY)

BAYERN MUNICH

EREDIVISIE (HOLLAND)

AJAX

A PFG (BULGARIA)

LUDOGORETS RAZGRAD

PRVA HNL (CROATIA)

DINAMO ZAGREB

GAMBRINUS LIGA (CZECH REPUBLIC)

SPARTA PRAGUE

SUPERLIGA (DENMARK)

AaB FODBOLD

VEIKKAUSLIIGA (FINLAND)

(2013) HJK HELSINKI

PREMIER LEAGUE (ISRAEL)

MACCABI TEL AVIV

SUPERLEAGUE (GREECE)

OLYMPIACOS

TIPPELIGAEN (NORWAY)

(2013) STROMSGODSET IF

PRIMEIRA LIGA (PORTUGAL)
BENFICA

EKSTRAKLASA (POLAND)
LEGIA WARSAW

PREMIER LEAGUE (RUSSIA)
CSKA MOSCOW

LIGA 1 (ROMANIA)
STEAUA BUCURESTI

SUPERLIGA (SERBIA)
RED STAR

CORGON LIGA (SLOVAKIA)
SK SLOVAN BRATISLAVA

MLS (USA)
(2013) SPORTING KANSAS CITY

CANADIAN SOCCER LEAGUE (CANADA)
(2013) SC WATERLOO REGION

LIGA MX (MEXICO)
CLUB LEON

CAMPEONATO BRASILEIRO SERIE A (BRAZIL)
CRUZEIRO

PRIMERA DIVISION (ARGENTINA)
SAN LORENZO

PRIMERA DIVISION (URUGUAY)
DANUBIO

J. LEAGUE DIVISION 1 (JAPAN)
(2013) SANFRECCE HIROSHIMA

K LEAGUE (SOUTH KOREA)
(2013) POHANG STEELERS

UAE ARABIAN GULF LEAGUE (UNITED ARAB EMIRATES)
AL-AHLI

LEAGUE: PREMIER LEAGUE (EGYPT)
(2011) AL AHLY

PREMIER SOCCER LEAGUE (SOUTH AFRICA)
MAMELODI SUNDOWNS

GHANA PREMIER LEAGUE (GHANA)
ASANTE KOTOKO

A-LEAGUE (AUSTRALIA)
BRISBANE ROAR

ASB PREMIERSHIP (NEW ZEALAND)
AUCKLAND CITY FC

EUROPE

NORTH AMERICA

SOUTH AMERICA

ASIA

AFRICA

OCEANIA

AARON RAMSEY

DID YOU KNOW?

As a schoolboy Ramsey was a keen rugby league player and was scouted by St Helens.

RAMSEY ON...

ARSENAL'S FA CUP WIN

"Being in the final and lifting the trophy at the end of it is what you work for all season. It's what you dream about doing since you were a young kid. I'm over the moon to score the winner but more importantly I'm over the moon to win the trophy and hopefully this will be the first of many."

ARSENE WENGER

"He has brought through so many great young players and turned them into world-class players. He gives youngsters opportunities and if he feels that you're good enough he'll play you so those factors were massive for me. He has been a big influence in my career so far."

CAREER MILESTONES

April 2007: Became Cardiff City's youngest ever player when he made his debut against Hull City in the Championshi, aged just 16 years and 124 days.

April 2008: Scored his first league goal for the Bluebirds in a 3-3 draw against Burnley

May 2008: FA Cup finalist with Cardiff

June, 2008: After an impressive season, Arsenal manager Arsene Wenger signed the Welshman for £4.8m

August 2008: Made his Arsenal debut against FC Twente in the Champions League qualifying round

October 2008: Became the fifth youngest scorer in Champions League history when he netted in the 5-2 win against Fenerbache

November 2008: Made his Wales debut against Denmark

August 2009: Scored his first Premier League goal in a 4-1 win against Portsmouth

February 2010: Suffered a double leg fracture against Stoke City.

March 2011: Captained his country for the first time against England.

July 2012 - Represented Great Britain at the Olympic Games

September 2013: Won the Premier League Player of the Month award after scoring four goals in four games.

May 2013: Scored the winner in Arsenal's FA Cup final victory over Hull City

FACT FILE

AARON RAMSEY

Position: Midfielder
Birth date: December 26, 1990
Birth place: Caerphilly, Wales
Height: 1.82m (6ft 0in)
Clubs: Cardiff City, Arsenal, Nottingham Forest (loan), Cardiff City (loan)
International: Wales

WHAT HIS BOSS SAYS

*"He has matured as a player and a person as well. I was a midfielder and I would have loved to have what he has. He can defend, attack and score goals. But I feel there's more to come. If he continues to play like that then he will have a very good future with the national side too." **Arsene Wenger.***

EXTRA TIME Former Arsenal midfielder Patrick Vieira described Ramsey as the best player in the Premier League in the first half of the 2013-14 season. The Frenchman made over 400 appearances for the Gunners and won three Premier League titles.

DELPH ON...

HIS FIRST PREMIER LEAGUE GOAL

"Last time I scored a goal like that was at Leeds, so it's nice to get off the mark. I've been getting a bit of stick from the lads (for not scoring), but I've now been given the licence to get forward and to get a few shots off."

VILLA'S YOUNG SQUAD

"We've got a lot of fire in our bellies. We won't sit down and we won't give up - we keep fighting for each other. It's a close-knit group. We're like brothers who fight every minute of every game."

CAREER MILESTONES

September 2001: Joined Leeds United's academy

May 2007: Made his Leeds debut as a substitute in a Championship match against Derby County

September 2008: Signed a new four-year deal with Leeds

September 2008: Scored his first senior goal against Crewe Alexandra

November 2008: He made his debut for the England Under-21's as a substitute against the Czech Republic

April 2009: Won the Football League Young Player of the Year and Leeds United's Players' player and Young Player of the Year awards

August 2009: Completed a £6m move to Premier League side Aston Villa

August 2009: Made his Premier League debut against Wigan Athletic

January 2010: Scored his first Villa goal against Brighton & Hove Albion in the FA Cup

April 2010: Suffered a cruciate ligament injury which kept him out of action for eight months

December 2013: Scored his first Premier League goal in a 3-2 win at Southampton

DID YOU KNOW?

Delph played 45 League One matches and only one Championship game before Aston Villa signed him for £6m.

FACT FILE

FABIAN DELPH

Position: Midfielder
Birth date: November 21, 1989
Birth place: Bradford, England
Height: 1.74m (5ft 9in)
Clubs: Leeds United, Aston Villa, Leeds United (loan)
International: England Under 21s

WHAT HIS BOSS SAYS

"I knew about his potential at Leeds because I'd seen him there. He's been excellent and he's got great energy so there's massive potential there to be a really top player. If he keeps his feet on the ground, keeps learning, keeps doing what he's doing then we'll see where he goes."
Paul Lambert.

EXTRA TIME Former Liverpool defender Jamie Carragher believes that Fabian Delph could be in line for an England call-up. The pundit made 38 appearances for the Three Lions.

SPOT THE BOSS!

All managers love a bargain buy player - someone they can pick up cheap and turn into a world beater. It's not easy finding those stars of tomorrow so many coaches and scouts sneak into games to watch their transfer targets.

CAN YOU FIND THE *SIX* TOP MANAGERS WHO HAVE HIDDEN IN THE CROWD?

FACES IN THE CROWD

BRENDAN RODGERS   ROY HODGSON   MANUEL PELLEGRINI

PAUL LAMBERT

MARK HUGHES

ROBERTO MARTÍNEZ

TRUE OR FALSE?

CAN YOU SORT THE FOOTBALL FACTS FROM THE FICTION?

1

ZLATAN IBRAHIMOVIC HAS WON LEAGUE TITLES IN FOUR DIFFERENT COUNTRIES

F T

2

QATAR WILL HOST THE 2018 WORLD CUP

F T

DAVID BECKHAM ENDED HIS CAREER PLAYING FOR PARIS SAINT-GERMAIN

F T

3

RYAN GIGGS NEVER PLAYED AT A MAJOR INTERNATIONAL TOURNAMENT

4

F T

5

WILLIAM CARVALHO PLAYS INTERNATIONAL FOOTBALL FOR BRAZIL

F T

6

THE 2015 CHAMPIONS LEAGUE FINAL WILL BE PLAYED AT WEMBLEY STADIUM

F T

7

WEST BROM MIDFIELDER CRAIG GARDNER STARTED HIS CAREER WITH RIVALS ASTON VILLA

F T

CHELSEA HAVE WON TWO PREMIER LEAGUE TITLES **8**

F T

BAYERN MUNICH MANAGER PEP GUARDIOLA USED TO CAPTAIN SPAIN **9**

F T

SOUTHAMPTON SIGNED FORWARD JAY RODRIGUEZ FROM BLACKBURN ROVERS **10**

F T

ENGLAND MANAGER ROY HODGSON STARTED HIS COACHING CAREER IN SWEDEN **11**

F T

LIVERPOOL STAR RAHEEM STERLING STARTED HIS YOUTH CAREER AT QUEENS PARK RANGERS **12**

F T

13 ARSENAL STAR SANTI CAZORLA PLAYS INTERNATIONAL FOOTBALL FOR SPAIN

F T

MANCHESTER CITY WERE EVERTON DEFENDER SYLVAIN DISTIN'S FIRST ENGLISH CLUB **14**

F T

15 ASHLEY COLE NEVER SCORED AN INTERNATIONAL GOAL IN HIS 107 CAPS FOR ENGLAND

F T

MEGA QUIZ
PART 1

Think you know all there is to know about the beautiful game? Here's your chance to show off your knowledge in the first half of our testing two-part quiz.

1 Manchester United manager Louis van Gaal is from which country?

2 Who scored Real Madrid's equaliser in the 2014 Champions League final?

3  Where do Queens Park Rangers play their home matches?

4 How many Everton players were in England's World Cup squad?

18   78

5 In 2014, which League 2 club lost in the play-offs for the second consecutive year?

6 In which country do Boca Juniors play their football?

CABJ

7 Who did Brazil play against in the opening game of the 2014 World Cup?

9 Which club narrowly avoided relegation from the Championship thanks to a last minute goal in 2013-14.

9 Arsenal won the 2014 FA Cup, but who did they beat in the semi-finals?

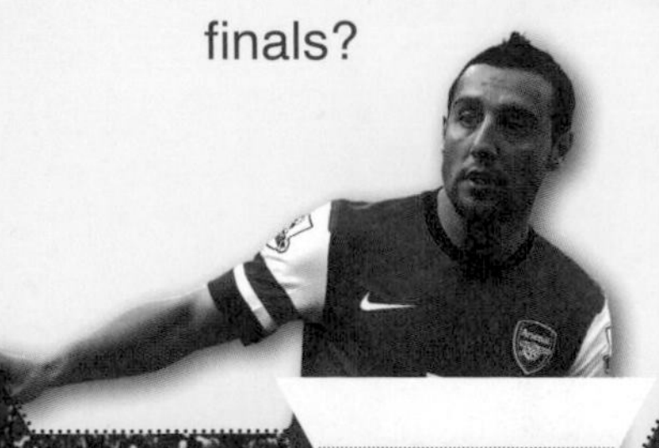

10 What is Norwich City's nickname?

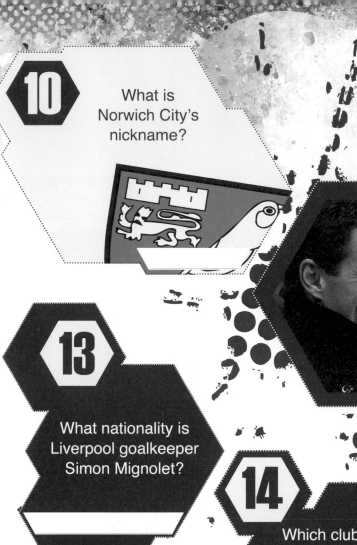

11 Who did Gus Poyet replace as Sunderland manager?

12 Sheffield United play their football in which league?

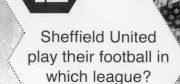

13 What nationality is Liverpool goalkeeper Simon Mignolet?

14 Which club ended FC Porto's five-and-a-half-year unbeaten home record?

15 How many Premier League clubs did Craig Bellamy play for?

WHO AM I?

CLUB: Leicester City
POSITION: Goalkeeper

CLUB: Stoke
POSITION: Midfielder

CLUB: Real Madrid
POSITION: Forward

CLUB: Man City
POSITION: Defender

CLUB: Liverpool
POSITION: Midfielder

SHIRT SWAP

GARETH BALE

ALEX OXLADE-CHAMBERLAIN

NIGEL DE JONG

ZLATAN IBRAHIMOVIC

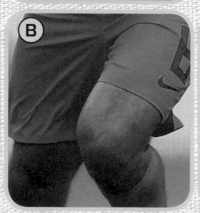

SHIRT	✓	SHIRT	✓	SHIRT	✓	SHIRT	✓
SHORTS	✓	SHORTS	✓	SHORTS	✓	SHORTS	✓
SOCKS	✓	SOCKS	✓	SOCKS	✓	SOCKS	✓

The kit man has had a very bad day and handed these superstars the wrong international shirt, shorts and socks. Can you help out by connecting each player with their right kit so they are ready to enter the pitch and entertain the crowd.

ANDRES INIESTA

MESUT OZIL

ROBERT SNODGRASS

PAUL POGBA

SHIRT SHORTS SOCKS

SHIRT SHORTS SOCKS

SHIRT SHORTS SOCKS

SHIRT SHORTS SOCKS

CITY'S WARRIOR

CITY'S WARRIOR

FACT FILE

VINCENT KOMPANY
POSITION: CENTRE-BACK
BIRTH DATE: APRIL 10, 1986
PLACE OF BIRTH: UCCLE, BRUSSELS,
BELGIUM
HEIGHT: 1.93M (6FT 4IN)
INTERNATIONAL: BELGIUM

KOMPANY AIMING TO BUILD ON SUCCESS

Vincent Kompany has had another magnificent year in the blue and white of Manchester City. The super skipper guided his side to a second Premier League title as they pipped Liverpool and Chelsea to the trophy. The Belgium star, who captained his country at the World Cup in Brazil, also lifted the League Cup in what was a highly successful first season under manager Manuel Pellegrini. But there's bad news for City's rivals as Kompany tells Shoot that the Etihad outfit, who scored 156 goals in all competitions in 2013-14, can only get better.

WHERE DOES WINNING THE DOUBLE RANK IN YOUR CAREER?

"Leading Man City to the league and cup double is probably the proudest moment in my career so far. The end of the season couldn't have ended any better."

WHAT DID IT MEAN TO THE CLUB TO WIN BACK THE TROPHY?

"It is what I wanted. It felt like an achievement – a huge achievement. When I started at City I would never have thought we would have all those trophies by now, but after we won the first one, I just wanted this to carry on. The rate in which we win trophies – I want this to increase. For me, it's still a long-term project. We've won the league and the League Cup, but they are just building blocks for the future."

HOW WAS LAST SEASON?

"I've been playing in England for a number of years now, so I know how hard you have to work in order to get the results that the club and the fans have come to expect. We all did our bit last season, sticking together through the defeats and disappointment led us to a successful season with a great team spirit and camaraderie."

WHAT'S IT LIKE TO WORK FOR MANUEL PELLEGRINI?

"The positive thing is that we'd won trophies before Pellegrini, but we've won trophies with him, so you can see we're carrying on with our winning habit. He's obviously got his own playing style and his style is very, very good for offensive minded players like Samir Nasri and others."

HOW IMPORTANT HAVE THE FORWARDS BEEN AS YOU SCORED AN INCREDIBLE 156 GOALS IN ALL COMPETITIONS LAST TERM?

"It's true they were incredible for us last season, they were so important. I can only say that I'm happy with that because this is the way football should be played, and if you win stuff as well then you are doing something right. It's fantastic that our forward minded players are coming into the game so well. As long as we keep winning I'm, and the rest of us, are always going to be happy."

WHAT'S THE AIM FOR 2014-15?

"Our aim is to build and maintain on last season's success. You can always improve and that's something we strive for in training every day. Each competition that we now enter, we want to win. It's a great time to be a player at Manchester City and I'm thoroughly enjoying it here."

YAYA TOURE SCORED 24 GOALS IN 2013-14. HOW GOOD IS HE?

"I don't think you need me to tell you. Twenty goals from midfield in a fiercely competitive league like ours is an incredible achievement. For me he is one of the best players in the world and we are lucky to have him at Manchester City."

WHY HAVE THE CLUB FOUND THE CHAMPIONS LEAGUE MORE DIFFICULT THAN MANY EXPECTED?

"It's a good question that we as players all want to put right. I feel we were unlucky not to progress from the group stages in our first couple of years in the competition. We are now beginning to expect more from ourselves in the Champions League. As I say, in every competition we enter, we want to do well and win it."

HOW SPECIAL WAS IT TO CAPTAIN BELGIUM AT THE WORLD CUP?

"To captain my country is always special, but in Brazil, where they are so passionate about their football, made it that extra special. Playing in a World Cup is something I've always dreamt about ever since I was a young child. As a kid playing with my friends on the streets we'd imagine playing for Belgium, calling out names who were part of the national set-up at the time. To actually do that for real in Rio and be captain was the greatest honour a player can experience. It's what dreams are made of."

WHAT THEY SAY

"THERE ARE SOME LEADERS WHO LEAD OTHERS WITH HOW THEY PLAY AND OTHERS WITH WORDS, BUT FOR VINNY IT IS BOTH. THIS IS WHY HE IS THE CAPTAIN OF CITY AND BELGIUM. THIS IS BECAUSE HE ALWAYS FIGHTS FOR THE TEAM, SHOWS PASSION AND LIKES TO TALK." SAMIR NASRI, MANCHESTER CITY TEAM-MATE.

DID YOU KNOW?

KOMPANY MADE HIS INTERNATIONAL DEBUT FOR BELGIUM AT THE AGE OF 17 IN 2004.

AROUND THE WORLD

K **A** **D** **M** **J** **P** **F** **N** **L** **C** **B** **H** **O**

EDINSON CAVANI
FORWARD ⚪

SHINJI KAGAWA
MIDFIELDER ⚪

Think you know your football and countries? Well here's a challenge for you! We've listed 16 top players from around the world. Your job is to match them up with the country they play for. Good luck!

DIDIER DROGBA
STRIKER ⚪

ALAN DZAGOEV
MIDFIELDER ⚪

MILE JEDINAK
MIDFIELDER ⚪

NEYMAR
FORWARD ⚪

CHRIS WOOD
STRIKER ⚪

GERARD PIQUE
DEFENDER

ALEX SONG
MIDFIELDER

MOHAMED SALAH
FORWARD

I

G

E

GARY CAHILL
DEFENDER

CLINT DEMPSEY
FORWARD

NURI SAHIN
MIDFIELDER

GIOVANI DOS SANTOS
FORWARD

ROBERT LEWANDOWSKI
STRIKER

KARIM BENZEMA
STRIKER

FERNANDINHO
MANCHESTER CITY AND BRAZIL

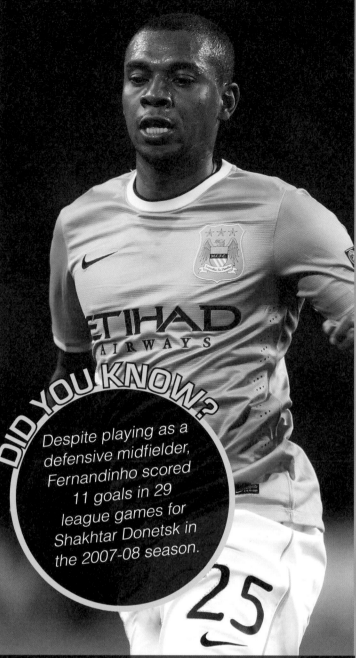

DID YOU KNOW?

Despite playing as a defensive midfielder, Fernandinho scored 11 goals in 29 league games for Shakhtar Donetsk in the 2007-08 season.

FACT FILE

FERNANDINHO

Position: Central midfielder
Birth date: May 4, 1985
Birth place: Londrina, Brazil
Height: 1.75m (5ft 9in)
Clubs: Atletico Paranaense, Shakhtar Donetsk, Manchester City
International: Brazil

WHAT HIS BOSS SAYS

"I made signing Fernandinho one of the top priorities. "He is a superb athlete with a wide range of passing, can score goals and most importantly, can quickly turn defence into attack." Manuel Pellegrini.

FERNANDINHO ON...

WINNING THE PREMIER LEAGUE

"To win the Premier League is amazing, and in the first season it is doubly amazing. I am so happy, I am so glad to help my team, and I am so proud to play for this team."

MANUEL PELLEGRINI

"Pellegrini is always calm, if you have problems he will try to resolve it. For me he's a special manager. He has the group in his hands - and the group play for him."

CAREER MILESTONES

April 2003: Made his debut as a 17-year-old for Atletico Paranaense
December 2003: Scored the winning goal for Brazil in the FIFA World Youth Championship final against a Spain side featuring Andres Iniesta
July 2005: Moved to Shakhtar Donetsk for £7m
May 2006: Wins his first of six Ukrainian Premier League titles
May 2009: Wins the UEFA Cup after Shakhtar beat Werder Bremen 2-1 in the final in Istanbul
August 2011: Made his international debut for Brazil against Germany at the age of 26
June 2013: Signed for Manchester City for a fee of around £30m
December 2013: Scored his first two goals for Manchester City in a 6-3 win at home against Arsenal
March 2014: Wins his first trophy as a Manchester City player with the club beating Sunderland 3-1 in the League Cup final
March 2014: Scores his first goal at international level in a 5-0 friendly win against South Africa
May 2014: Wins the Premier League title

EXTRA TIME The Brazilian became one of the most successful foreign players to appear in the Ukrainian Premier League after winning six league titles, four Cups and three Super Cups.

ERIKSEN ON...

SPURS

"Everyone has followed the development of Spurs and it's something I wanted to be part of. I read about the history of Spurs and had seen games over the years. I knew a bit about the club - they like a bit of creativity."

HIS POSITION

"I'm really enjoying playing right now – it doesn't matter where. I love playing. If I get a chance I try to take it and it doesn't depend on where I play, it just depends on where the spaces are and where I can get the ball."

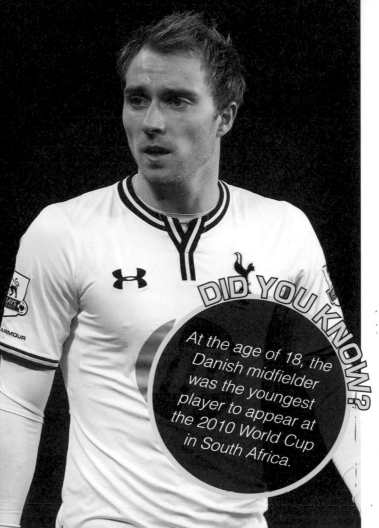

DID YOU KNOW?

At the age of 18, the Danish midfielder was the youngest player to appear at the 2010 World Cup in South Africa.

CAREER MILESTONES

January 2010: Made his Ajax debut for the first team against NAC Breda

March 2010: Scored his first goal for the club in a 6-0 win against Go Ahead Eagles in the Dutch Cup

May 2010: Wins his first silverware as Ajax beat Feyenoord in the Dutch Cup final

March 2010: First senior cap for Denmark

May 2010: Named in Denmark's 2010 World Cup final squad

June 2010: Makes his first World Cup appearance against the Netherlands.

May 2011: Wins the first of three Eredivisie titles

May 2011: Named Dutch Football Talent of the Year.

June 2011: Scored his first Denmark goal against Iceland in a Euro 2012 qualifier

October 2011: Scored his first Champions League goal against Dinamo Zagreb

August 2013: Signs for Tottenham Hotspur for £11m.

September 2013: Makes his Tottenham debut in the Premier League against Norwich City.

September 2013: Scored his first Tottenham goal against Tromso in the Europa League

December 2013: Scored his first Premier League goal against West Bromwich Albion

FACT FILE

CHRISTIAN ERIKSEN

Position: Midfielder

Birth date: February 14, 1992

Birth place: Middelfart, Denmark

Height: 1.77m (5ft 10in)

Clubs: Ajax, Tottenham Hotspur

International: Denmark

WHAT THEY SAY

"Christian Eriksen is one of the best acquisitions that this club has ever made. He's a fantastic trainer, has so much in the locker. He not only assists he scores, he affects football matches." *Tim Sherwood, ex-Tottenham boss.*

WHAT HIS TEAM-MATE SAYS

"He is a brilliant player. He is a player who is capable of improving all of us. He is a player that makes everything look easy and that's good for us. He can offer us a lot of passes to everyone who plays in attack for Spurs." *Roberto Soldado*

EXTRA TIME *When former Arsenal striker Dennis Bergkamp worked with Eriksen at Ajax he said that the midfielder had it all. Bergkamp scored 120 goals in 423 appearances for the Gunners.*

GROUND GAME

The biggest and best stadiums can be easily recognised around the world. They are the theatres of football and every fan will view their home ground as a second home. But how much do you know about football grounds. Take a look at the images and match each one to the name of the stadium, which club plays there and its crowd capacity.

Ground:

Team:

Capacity:

Ground:

Team:

Capacity:

Ground:

Team:

Capacity:

Ground:

Team:

Capacity:

Ground:

Team:

Capacity:

Ground:

Team:

Capacity:

Ground:

Team:

Capacity:

Ground:

Team:

Capacity:

Ground:

Team:

Capacity:

Ground:

Team:

Capacity:

Ground:

Team:

Capacity:

Ground:

Team:

Capacity:

Ground:

Team:

Capacity:

Ground:

Team:

Capacity:

Ground:

Team:

Capacity:

GROUNDS

Goodison Park	Villa Park
St James' Park	Bernabeu
White Hart Lane	Allianz Arena
Camp Nou	Stade Velodrome
Westfalenstadion	St Mary's
San Siro	Estádio do Dragåo
Maracana	
The Valley	
Elland Road	

TEAM:

Tottenham Hotspur	Bayern Munich
Barcelona	Newcastle United
Borussia Dortmund	Marseille
Flamengo	A.C. Milan
FC Porto	Southampton
Charlton Athletic	Everton
Leeds United	
Aston Villa	
Real Madrid	

CAPACITY:

52,405	71,437
32,589	48,000
36,284	40,157
80,700	52,399
78,838	80,018
27,111	81,044
39,460	
42,682	
99,354	

DEADLY DANIEL

STURRIDGE'S SUPER YEAR

AFTER A STUTTERING START TO HIS CAREER DANIEL STURRIDGE HAS FINALLY ESTABLISHED HIMSELF AS A TOP CLASS STRIKER.

The Birmingham-born star struck 21 Premier League goals in 29 appearances for Liverpool in the 2013-14 season to help the Reds qualify for the Champions League and finish second, just two points behind winners Manchester City.

His form earned him a deserved call-up to Roy Hodgson's England squad for the World Cup in Brazil where he showed why he was handed the number 9 shirt by scoring the Three Lions' first goal of the tournament in a 2-1 defeat to Italy.

But the forward's path to the top was definitely not straightforward.

After leaving Manchester City for Chelsea as a talented teenager in 2009, he was restricted to just two league starts in 18 months before moving to Bolton Wanderers on loan.

It was at the Reebok where the sharp shooter started to show he has what it takes to succeed in the Premier League, scoring eight times in 12 appearances for the Trotters.

This made the then Chelsea boss Andre Villas-Boas sit up and take notice, as Sturridge started to force his way into the starting line-up at Stamford Bridge.

However, Villas-Boas and then Roberto Di Matteo were deploying the speed demon on the right wing – an unfamiliar position to the natural centre forward.

Despite having collected a Champions League winners' medal in May 2012,

more time on the flanks and on the bench saw another frustrating six months tick by at the start of the following campaign.

But then came Sturridge's big break - a £12m transfer to Liverpool in January 2013.

And the goal getter got off to a flying start at Anfield, scoring against Manchester United on his debut before hitting the net a further nine times in 13 matches to give the Reds faithful a taste of what was to come the following season.

The 2013-14 campaign was the first time Sturridge hit the 20-goal mark since turning professional in a year that saw him form a brilliant and deadly 52-goal partnership with Luis Suarez – dubbed SAS.

It wasn't quite enough to grab Liverpool their first Premier League title but it's a year that announced Daniel Sturridge to the world. The bad news for defenders is that there's plenty more to come.

LIVERPOOL

"I'm humbled and happy to be here. It's a humongous club - for me, one of the biggest in the world. To have the fans and world-class players we have here is amazing."

LAST SEASON

"We're all hungry for success and the fans deserve success. They've given us great support from the first minute to the last and I apologise to them for not winning the Premier League."

PLAYING AT THE WORLD CUP

"In a sense, I lived my dream. It's the number one highlight of my career because it's been a long journey for myself and my family."

BRENDAN RODGERS

"Tactically, he's the best [manager] I have worked with. From a man-management point of view, he's always pushing to get the best out of me."

STEVEN GERRARD

"He is a legend and a great man on and off the pitch too. He deserves everything he gets because he works hard and he is someone everyone looks up to. He is a leader and the captain of the boys."

WHAT THEY SAY...

"Daniel has turned into a top, top striker and it's great to see. Brendan Rodgers deserves a lot of credit for his progress. He didn't get a chance at Chelsea but went to Liverpool and played almost every game. His goalscoring record is incredible. He's unpredictable and that makes him hard to mark for defenders. That's a quality of his." **Wayne Rooney, England team-mate.**

MILESTONES

February 2007: Senior debut for Manchester City versus Reading.

January 2008: First senior goal versus Sheffield United (FA Cup)
First Premier League goal versus Derby County

April 2008: Wins FA Youth Cup

May 2009: Voted Manchester City's Young Player of the Year

July 2009: Signed for Chelsea

August 2009: Chelsea debut versus Sunderland

January 2010: First Chelsea goal versus Watford

April 2010: First Chelsea Premier League goal versus Stoke City

May 2010: Won a Premier League and FA Cup winners' medal with Chelsea

September 2010: Scored on Champions League debut versus MSK Zilina

January 2011: Signed for Bolton on loan

February 2011: Scored on Bolton debut versus Wolverhampton Wanderers

November 2011: Made England debut versus Sweden

May 2012: Won a Champions League and FA Cup winners' medal with Chelsea

July 2012: Made Great Britain debut at the Olympic Games

August 2012: Scored his first Great Britain goal versus United Arab Emirates

January 2013: Completed a £12m transfer to Liverpool

January 2013: Scored on Liverpool debut versus Mansfield Town

March 2013: Scored first England goal versus San Marino.

January 2013: Scored on Liverpool Premier League debut versus Manchester United

February 2014: Scored 50th Premier League goal

April 2014: Named in the PFA Team of the Year
Scores 20th Premier League goal of the season

May 2014: Named in England's World Cup squad

June 2014: Scored on World Cup debut versus Italy

FACT FILE

Daniel Sturridge

Position: Striker
Date of Birth: September 1, 1989
Place of Birth: Birmingham, England
Height: 1.83m (6ft 0in)
Clubs: Manchester City, Chelsea, Bolton Wanderers (loan), Liverpool
International: England

GOALS

Manchester City
2006-07 Games: 2 Goals: 0
2007-08 Games: 4 Goals: 2
2008-09 Games: 26 Goals: 4
Chelsea
2009-10 Games: 21 Goals: 5
2010-11 Games: 20 Goals: 4
2011-12 Games: 43 Goals:13
2012-13 Games: 12 Goals: 2
Bolton (loan)
2010-11 Games: 12 Goals: 8
Liverpool
2012-13 Games: 16 Goals: 11
2103-14 Games: 33 Goals: 24

DID YOU KNOW?

Sturridge is the only player ever to score in the FA Youth Cup, the FA Cup and the Premier League in the same season (2007-2008).

PHOTOFIT

The top plaers and managers in the beautiful game of football can now be recognised around the world. The face in each of the following four photos is made up of features from four England players/ super strikers/goalkeepers and managers. Your job is to spot whose head, eyes, nose and mouth make up the faces. Good luck!

HEAD

EYES

NOSE

MOUTH

2. SUPER STRIKERS

4. ENGLAND

HEAD

EYES

NOSE

MOUTH

3.KEEPERS

HEAD

EYES

NOSE

MOUTH

4.MANAGERS

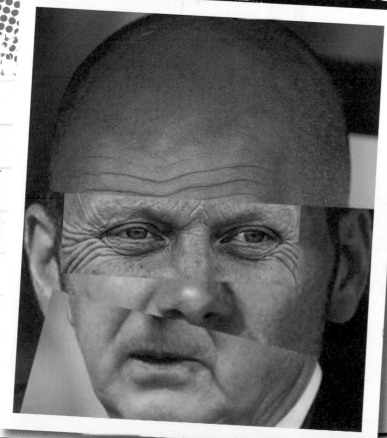

HEAD

EYES

NOSE

MOUTH

VURNON ANITA

NEWCASTLE UNITED AND NETHERLANDS

DID YOU KNOW?

Anita was named in the Netherlands' preliminary squad for the 2010 World Cup in South Affrica, but failed to make the final 23.

ANITA ON...

MOVING FROM AJAX TO NEWCASTLE

"I won almost everything in Holland so the step was not difficult to make. Now I think I can also win trophies with Newcastle and it's time to do that."

THE PREMIER LEAGUE

"English football is quicker, more direct and much more physical than the Dutch league. There is more long ball and fight, so it is different. That means I must do extra work to make me stronger because that will help me in games."

CAREER MILESTONES

March 2006: Made his Ajax debut in a Eredivisie against FC Groningen
May 2006: Won the first of three KNVB Cups
February 2007: Made his European debut in a 3-0 loss to Werder Bremen in the UEFA Cup
May 2010: Made his full debut for the Netherlands against Mexico.
May 2011: Won his first of two Eredivisie titles
August 2012: Signed for Newcastle United for a fee of £6.7m
August 2012: Made his debut as a substitute against Tottenham Hotspur in the Premier League
November 2012: Scored his first goal for the club against Club Brugge in the Europa League
March 2014: Scored his first Premier League goal for the club in the 4-1 win at Hull City

FACT FILE

VURNON ANITA
Position: Midfielder
Birth date: April 4, 1989
Birth place: Willemstad, Netherlands Antilles
Height: 1.68m (5ft 6in)
Clubs: Ajax, Newcastle United
International: Netherlands

WHAT THEY SAY

"*Vurnon is a stocky but sturdy man. Using his ferocity, he quickly puts pressure on his opponents at the right time. That is his greatest strength. You know that whatever job you ask him to do he will give you every ounce of sweat he's got.*"
Frank de Boer, Anita's boss at Ajax.

EXTRA TIME Despite making the central midfield role his primary position in recent years, Anita began his career as a left-back, and is comfortable with covering the full-back positions.

NOBLE ON...

LAST SEASON

"It has been tough but we have finished 13th and we were second from bottom in December. It is a credit to the lads and everyone involved in the club that we got ourselves out of that."

SAM ALLARDYCE

"I support the Gaffer because I have played every single game under Sam since he has come. I've always said to anyone who has asked me about the Gaffer that he has never asked me to boot it. I always try to get on the ball and make us play as much as possible and that's what has been happening."

CAREER MILESTONES

February 2003: Became the youngest player to appear for West Ham's reserve team
August 2004: Made his first-team debut for West Ham against Southend in the League Cup
May 2005: Won the West Ham's Young Hammer of the Year award
Promoted to the Premier League following a play-off final win against Preston North End
August 2005: Made his Premier League debut in a 3-1 win over Blackburn Rovers
February 2006: Joined Hull City on a three-month loan deal
August 2006: Joined Ipswich Town on a three-month loan deal
January 2007: Scored his first West Ham goal in a 3-0 win against Brighton & Hove Albion
June 2007: Made his England Under-21 debut against Slovakia
September 2007: Scored his first goal for England Under-21's in a 2-0 win against Bulgaria
March 2009: Scored on his 100th game for West Ham in a 1-1 draw with Blackburn Rovers
June 2009: Captained England U-21s at the European Championship
February 2012: Captained West Ham for the first time
May 2012: Promoted with West Ham to the Premier League following a play-off final win against Blackpool
September 2012: Made his 200th appearance for the club

DID YOU KNOW?

Despite playing for the England youth sides, Noble is also eligible to play for Republic of Ireland as he has never played at senior international level.

FACT FILE

MARK NOBLE

Position: Midfielder
Birth date: May 8, 1987
Birth place: Canning Town, London, England
Height: 1.80m (5ft 11in)
Clubs: West Ham United, Hull City (loan), Ipswich Town (loan)
International: England Under-21s

WHAT HIS BOSS SAYS

"It's about what's in Mark's blood. He's born and bred in the area and he's West Ham to the core. When you have players like that it gives the player a greater feeling every time he plays because it's his boyhood dream becoming reality."
Sam Allardyce.

EXTRA TIME Mark Noble captained the England Under-21s in the European Championship final in 2009 where England lost 4-0 to Germany.

SPOT THE DIFFERENCE!

WEST HAM v LIVERPOOL

Two pictures from two big matches - and our clever designer has made SIX changes to each. Spot the differences from picture A to picture B in each case and draw circles around the changes. Remember it might not always be the players that have changed. Good luck!

MAN UNITED v ASTON VILLA

DREAM TEAM

GK (Goalkeeper)

- **Iker Casillas** (Spain)
- **Joe Hart** (England)
- **Thibaut Courtois** (Belgium)

RB (Right Back)

- **Philipp Lahm** (Germany)
- **Dani Alves** (Brazil)
- **Glen Johnson** (England)
- •

LB (Left Back)

- **Patrice Evra** (France)
- **Jordi Alba** (Spain)
- **David Alaba** (Austria)

CB (Centre Back)

- **Thiago Silva** (Brazil)
- **Gerard Pique** (Spain)
- **Vincent Kompany** (Belgium)
- **Pepe** (Portugal)

There are so many great players in the modern game that it's hard to choose a best XI. So we've tried to help you out by selecting a squad of world-class players. As manager, all you have to do is pick your favourites from each position to make up your Shoot dream team.

DM (Defensive Midfield)

- **Andrea Pirlo** (Italy)
- **Xavi** (Spain)
- **Nigel de Jong** (Holland)

RF (Right Forward)

- **Lionel Messi** (Argentina)
- **Theo Walcott** (England)
- **Alexis Sanchez** (Chile)

LF (Left Forward)

- **Cristiano Ronaldo** (Portugal)
- **Neymar** (Brazil)
- **Gareth Bale** (Wales)

CM (Centre Midfield)

- **Yaya Toure** (Ivory Coast)
- **Andres Iniesta** (Spain)
- **Steven Gerrard** (England)
- **Mesut Ozil** (Germany)

ST (Striker)

- **Zlatan Ibrahimovic** (Sweden)
- **Wayne Rooney** (England)
- **Luis Suarez** (Uruguay)

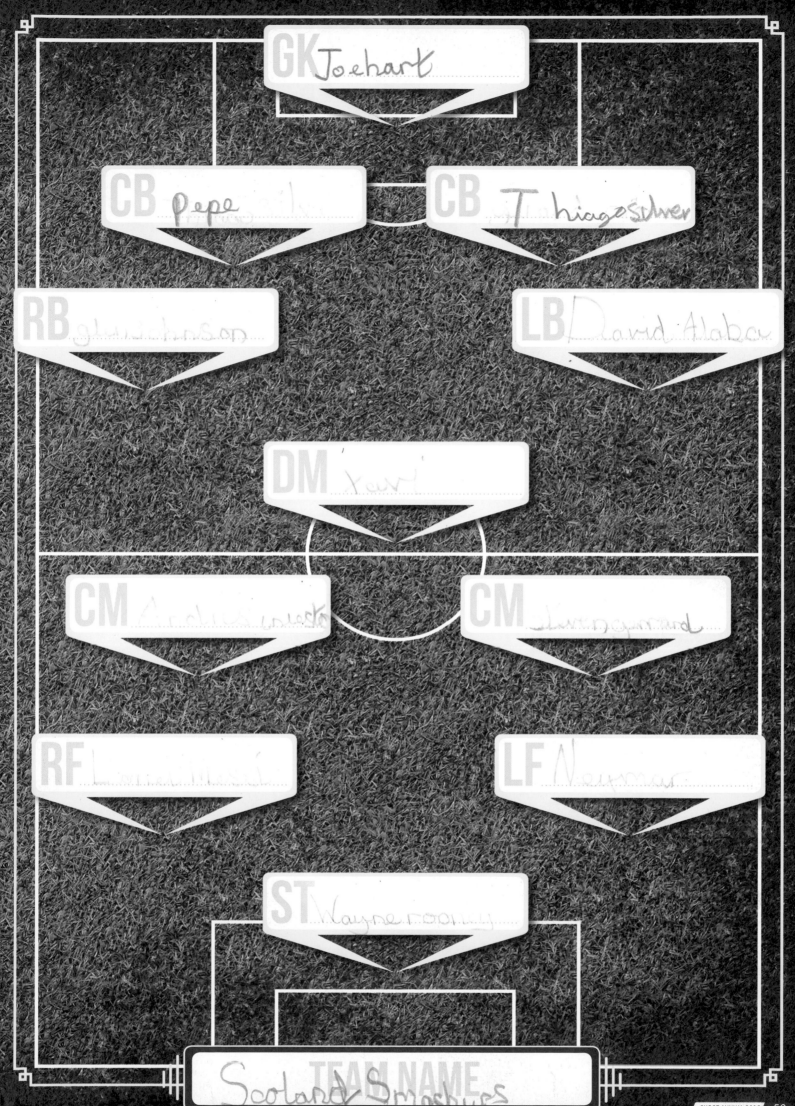

GK Joe hart

CB Pepe **CB** Thiago silver

RB g hutchnson **LB** David Alaba

DM Yaya

CM Andres iniesta **CM** Jurgen pmand

RF Lionel Messi **LF** Naymar

ST Wayne rooney

TEAM NAME Scotland Smashers

MONEY, M£NEY, MONEY

THE CLUBS, PLAYERS AND MANAGERS ROLLING IN CASH

CLUBS (MOST VALUABLE)

1. **Real Madrid** (Spain)	- £1.96 bn
2. **Manchester United** (England)	- £1.88 bn
3. **Barcelona** (Spain)	- £1.55 bn
4. **Arsenal** (England)	- £792 m
5. **Bayern Munich** (Germany)	- £779 m
6. **AC Milan** (Italy)	- £563 m
7. **Chelsea** (England)	- £536 m
8. **Juventus** (Italy)	- £413 m
9. **Manchester City** (England)	- £410 m
10. **Liverpool** (England)	- £388 m

MANAGERS (YEARLY SALARY)

1. **Jose Mourinho** (Chelsea)	- £13.98 m
2. **Pep Guardiola** (Bayern Munich)	- £12.34 m
3. **Roberto Mancini** (Galatasaray)	- £11.51 m
4. **Carlo Ancelotti** (Real Madrid)	- £11.10 m
5. **Fabio Capello** (Russia national team)	- £9.87 m
6. **Marcello Lippi** (Guangzhou Evergrande)	- £9.46 m
7. **Arsene Wenger** (Arsenal)	- £7.89 m
8. **Roberto Di Matteo** (unemployed – still being paid by Chelsea)	- £6.74 m
9. **Andre Villas-Boas** (Zenit St Petersburg – still being paid by Tottenham Hotspur)	- £5.67 m
10. **Rafael Benitez** (Napoli)	- £5.59 m

PLAYERS (YEARLY SALARY)

1. **Lionel Messi** (Barcelona)	- £31.1m
2. **Cristiano Ronaldo** (Real Madrid)	- £30.16 m
3. **Wayne Rooney** (Manchester United)	- £15.5 m
- **Gareth Bale** (Real Madrid)	- £15.5 m
5. **Radamel Falcao** (AS Monaco)	- £11.4 m
6. **Zlatan Ibrahimovic** (Paris Saint-Germain)	- £11.3 m
7. **Sergio Aguero** (Manchester City)	- £9.87 m
8. **Yaya Toure** (Manchester City)	- £9.46 m
9. **Thiago Silva** (Paris Saint-Germain)	- £9.8 m
- **David Silva** (Manchester City)	- £9.8 m

FIGURES ARE BEFORE TAX AND CORRECT AT THE END OF THE 2013-14 SEASON

WORLD'S BIGGEST STADIUMS
THE LARGEST GROUNDS ON THE PLANET

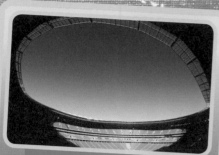

AFRICA
FNB STADIUM
WHERE: JOHANNESBURG, SOUTH AFRICA
TEAM: SOUTH AFRICA NATIONAL TEAM AND KAIZER CHIEFS
CAPACITY: 94,736
OPENED: 1989

ASIA
RUNGNADO MAY DAY STADIUM
WHERE: PYONGYANG, NORTH KOREA
TEAM: NORTH KOREA NATIONAL TEAM
CAPACITY: 150,000
OPENED: 1989

NORTH AMERICA
ESTADIO AZTECA
WHERE: MEXICO CITY, MEXICO
TEAM: MEXICO NATIONAL TEAM AND CLUB AMÉRICA
CAPACITY: 105,064
OPENED: 1966

SOUTH AMERICA
ESTADIO MONUMENTAL
WHERE: LIMA, PERU
TEAM: CLUB UNIVERSITARIO DE DEPORTES
CAPACITY: 80,093
OPENED: 2000

EUROPE
CAMP NOU
WHERE: BARCELONA, SPAIN
TEAM: FC BARCELONA
CAPACITY: 99,786
OPENED: 1957

AUSTRALIA
ANZ STADIUM
WHERE: SYDNEY, AUSTRALIA
TEAM: AUSTRALIA NATIONAL SIDE
CAPACITY: 83,500
OPENED: 1999

UK AND IRELAND – TOP 10

1. **90,000** – WEMBLEY STADIUM (ENGLAND)
2. **75,811** – OLD TRAFFORD (MANCHESTER UNITED)
3. **74,500** – MILLENNIUM STADIUM (WALES)
4. **60,355** – CELTIC PARK (CELTIC)
5. **60,338** – EMIRATES STADIUM (ARSENAL)
6. **52,405** – ST JAMES' PARK (NEWCASTLE UNITED)
7. **52,025** – HAMPDEN PARK (SCOTLAND)
8. **51,700** – AVIVA STADIUM (REPUBLIC OF IRELAND)
9. **50,987** – IBROX (RANGERS)
10. **49,000** – STADIUM OF LIGHT (SUNDERLAND)

DID YOU KNOW?

WEIRD, WACKY AND UNUSUAL FACTS ABOUT THE BEAUTIFUL GAME...

CLUB ATLÉTICO PARANAENSE
1924

BRAZILIAN FOOTBALLERS HAVE ALWAYS BEEN FAMOUS FOR THEIR WEIRD AND WACKY NAMES AND ONE OF THE LATEST BIG THINGS SET TO COME OUT OF BRAZIL IS MOSQUITO, WHO PLAYS AS A CENTRE FORWARD FOR ATLETICO PARANAENSE.

ALEX SONG HAS   SIBLINGS – 17 SISTERS AND 10 BROTHERS

POPE JOHN PAUL II NEARLY PLAYED PROFESSIONAL FOOTBALL

SIMON MIGNOLET CAN SPEAK FIVE DIFFERENT LANGUAGES AND HAS A DEGREE IN POLITICS

MANUEL NEUER STARRED IN THE GERMAN VERSION OF DISNEY PIXAR'S MONSTERS UNIVERSITY AS THE VOICE OF FRANK MCCAY

IN 2010, ROBERT LEWANDOWSKI ALMOST SIGNED FOR BLACKBURN ROVERS BUT A GIANT ASH CLOUD FROM ICELAND GROUNDED HIS PLANE AND DELAYED THE TRANSFER

RYAN GIGGS NEVER PICKED UP A RED CARD IN 672 PREMIER LEAGUE MATCHES

LUIS SUAREZ'S DAUGHTER IS CALLED DELFINA, WHICH IS AN ANAGRAM OF ANFIELD, DESPITE THE FACT THAT SHE WAS BORN SIX MONTHS BEFORE HE JOINED THE MERSEYSIDE CLUB.

STOKE GOALKEEPER ASMIR BEGOVIC SCORED THE SAME AMOUNT OF GOALS AS STRIKERS RICKY VAN WOLFSWINKEL AND JOZY ALTIDORE IN THE 2013-14 PREMIER LEAGUE SEASON

RUSSIA'S ALEKSANDR KOKORIN IS NICKNAMED BIEBER BECAUSE OF HIS LIKENESS TO THE CANADIAN POPSTAR.

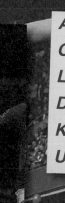

AROUND 10,000 PEOPLE (MAINLY TEENAGE GIRLS) TURNED OUT TO WATCH ONE DIRECTION'S LOUIS TOMLINSON MAKE AN APPEARANCE FOR DONCASTER ROVERS' RESERVES AT THE CLUB'S KEEPMOAT STADIUM. THE ATTENDANCE IS USUALLY AROUND 100.

CHELSEA DEFENDER CESAR AZPILICUETA HAS BEEN NICKNAMED 'DAVE' BECAUSE SO MANY PEOPLE WERE STRUGGLING TO PRONOUNCE HIS SURNAME.

MAYNOR FIGUEROA ONLY HAS THREE TOES ON HIS LEFT FOOT

LUKA MODRIC AND MARK VIDUKA ARE COUSINS

FIRST DIVISION BOLIVIAN CLUB SPORT BOYS SIGNED 54-YEAR-OLD PRESIDENT EVO MORALES TO PLAY AS A MIDFIELDER IN THE 2014-15 SEASON.

NAME — THAT YEAR

There's been many magical moments in the history of football that live long in the memory. Here are a number of memorable moments from the beautiful game. All you have to do is match each iconic image up with the year in which they happened. Good luck!

Barcelona beating Manchester United in the Champions League final

Bobby Moore lifting the World Cup for England

Diego Maradona's 'Hand of God' goal against England

Manchester City winning their first Premier League title

Manchester United's treble winning season

Blackburn Rovers win the Premier League

Carlos Tevez and Javier Mascherano sign for West Ham

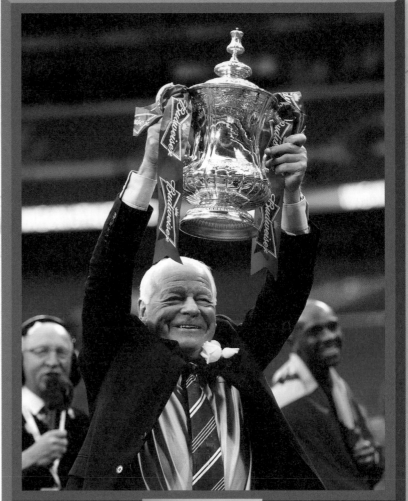

Wigan win the FA Cup

Arsenal go a whole season unbeaten

DATES	
1999	2013
1980	2011
2006	2012
2004	1966
1986	1995

Nottingham Forest win back-to-back European Cups

MEGA QUIZ
PART 2

Think you did well in the first half? Well now's the real test. Keep your concentration in the second half and you can rightfully call yourself a football know it all.

3 In which country did Arsene Wenger manage before taking over at Arsenal?

2 Which manager guided Rotherham to promotion in 2013 and 2014?

1 Which side ended their 50-year wait for a top flight title in 2005?

Who is the manager of the Republic of Ireland?

Where do Bristol City play their home matches?

5 Sir Bobby Charlton is England's record goalscorer with how many goals?

6

4

8 Which club did Liverpool sign Luis Suarez from?

7 Who did England play against in their opening 2014 World Cup match?

9 Where do Bayern Munich play their home matches?

In which country do Shakhtar Donetsk play their football?

11 Which north-east side play at the Riverside Stadium?

12 Who were the first British side to win the European Cup?

10

13 What nationality is Tottenham midfielder Erik Lamela?

14 Which two sides compete in the East Midlands Derby?

15 Jermain Defoe joined which MLS side in February 2014?

WHICH CLUB AM I?

NICKNAME: Gers
GROUND: Ibrox

NICKNAME: Rossoneri
GROUND: San Siro

NICKNAME: The Hammers
GROUND: Boleyn Ground

NICKNAME: Pompey
GROUND: Fratton Park

Nickname: Spurs
Ground: White Hart Lane

EDEN HAZARD
CHELSEA AND BELGIUM

DID YOU KNOW?

Eden comes from a footballing family, and his brother Thorgan also plays for Chelsea.

FACT FILE

Eden Hazard

Position: Forward
Birth date: January 7, 1991
Birth place: La Louvière, Belgium
Height: 1.70m (5ft 7in)
Clubs: Lille, Chelsea
International: Belgium

WHAT HIS BOSS SAYS

"If you ask me if I want Messi, Ronaldo or Neymar, I'd keep Hazard." Marc Wilmots, Belgium manager.

EXTRA TIME *French football legend Zinedine Zidane has heaped praised on Hazard, describing him as "special". The former Real Madrid midfielder won the FIFA World Player of the Year award on three occasions.*

HAZARD ON...

MOURINHO

"He lets people do their own thing, he gives a lot of confidence to his players, he motivates us with small statements, small sentences in the newspapers or face to face. I think I am giving that back to him on the pitch. As I often say, I hope it will last."

PRAISE

"I don't think I deserve it at the moment. To be thought of as one of the best five in the world, I would need to score more goals for a start. I would really need to score almost every game because that that is what the best players in the world - like Messi and Ronaldo - do every season. These are the guys everyone else has to aim for."

CAREER MILESTONES

November 2007: Made his professional debut for Lille in a friendly against Bruges
September 2008: Scored his first career goal which made him Lille's youngest ever scorer
November 2008: Made his international debut for Belgium as a substitute against Luxembourg
May 2011: Won the Coupe de France with Lille
Won the Ligue 1 title with Lille
Named Ligue 1 Player of the Year, making him the youngest player to ever win the award
October 2011: Scored his first international goal for Belgium in a 4-1 win over Kazakhstan
June 2012: Signed for Chelsea for £32m
August 2012: Made his Chelsea debut in the FA Community Shield
Scored his first goal for Chelsea in a 2-0 win over Newcastle in the Premier League
May 2013: Won the Europa League with Chelsea
February 2014: Scores first Chelsea hat-trick in 3-0 win over Newcastle

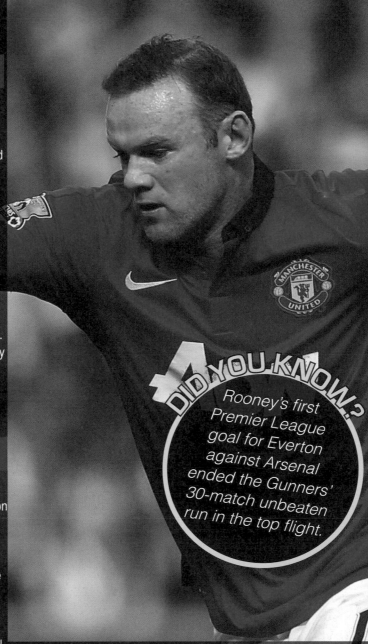

ROONEY ON...

HIS NEW CONTRACT

"This is one of the biggest clubs in the world and I've been here since I was 18. This contract will take me through to my thirties, which is almost my entire professional career. I've played most of my best football here and am looking forward to hopefully playing even better football in the next few years."

TRYING TO CATCH BOBBY CHARLTON'S CLUB SCORING RECORD OF 249

"It is definitely something I would like to achieve. If I managed to do it it'd be something I'd be very proud of. My aim is always to score and create as many goals as possible, so if I can continue to score regularly and break the record then I would be delighted."

CAREER MILESTONES

August 2002: Made his senior debut for Everton in the Premier League

October 2002: Scored his first professional goals in the League Cup

October 2002: Scored his first Premier League goal against Arsenal at the age of 16

February 2003: Made his England debut against Australia

September 2003: Scored his first England goal against Macedonia

August 2004: Joined Manchester United for a fee in the region of £27m

September 2004: Scored a hat-trick on his debut against Fenerbache

May 2007: Won his first of five Premier League titles

May 2008: Won the Champions League after United beat Chelsea on penalties

August 2009: Scored his 100th goal for the club

November 2009: Captained England for the first time

January 2010: Scored his 100th Premier League goal

April 2010: Won the PFA Players' Player of the Year Award

October 2012: Became England's fifth highest ever goalscorer

September 2013: Scored his 200th goal for the club

February 2014: Signed a new five-and-a-half year deal worth £300,000 a week

DID YOU KNOW? Rooney's first Premier League goal for Everton against Arsenal ended the Gunners' 30-match unbeaten run in the top flight.

FACT FILE

Wayne Rooney

Position: Striker

Birth date: October 24, 1985

Birth place: Liverpool, England

Height: 1.76m (5ft 9in)

Clubs: Everton, Manchester United

International: England

WHAT HIS TEAM-MATE SAYS

"He has a bit of everything. He can drop, he can go behind, he can play the short game, longer game. We are helping each other out. We both play behind and a bit higher up. It seems to be working well. I love playing with Wayne." *Robin van Persie.*

EXTRA TIME *Rooney needs 10 goals to surpass Sir Bobby Charlton's all-time goalscoring record for England. The striker netted his 40th international goal in June to put him nine behind the 1966 World Cup winner and United legend.*

YOU DECIDE WHICH FLYING FORWARD'S THE BEST

HEADING:

DETERMINATION:

CLUB: REAL MADRID

DOB: 16.07.1989

HEIGHT: 1.83 M (6 FT 0IN)

POWER:

TACKLING:

FITNESS:

SET PIECES:

DRIBBLING:

BALANCE:

PACE:

PREVIOUS CLUBS:
SOUTHAMPTON

TOTTENHAM HOTSPUR

INTERNATIONAL:
WALES

GARETH BALE
FORWARD

SHOOTING:

BIRTH PLACE:
CARDIFF, WALES

DID YOU KNOW?
Bale became just the third player to win the PFA Player and Young Player of the Year Awards in 2013.

WHAT THEY SAY...
"He is one of the best I have ever witnessed. He is an unbelievable player, he really is. He is a fantastic weapon for us."
Chris Coleman, Wales boss.

TOTAL: / 110

SKILL:

EXTRA TIME

Bale was Wales' youngest player when he made his international debut at the age of 16 years and 315 days in 2006.

Despite currently living in the large shadows of club team-mates Lionel Messi and Cristiano Ronaldo, Neymar and Gareth Bale can also be regarded as two of the world's best players.

Barcelona paid a staggering £71m for Brazil's golden boy, while Real Madrid splashed out a world-record £85m on Welsh wing wizard, Bale.

The deadly duo have put in world class performances for both club and country in their short careers to date, but who do you think is the best?

Mark each of their skills out of 10 and add up the total to see which awesome superstar comes out on top in the battle of the El Clasico attackers.

CLUB: BARCELONA

DOB: 5.02.1992

HEIGHT: 1.75M (5FT 9IN)

HEADING:

TACKLING:

DETERMINATION:

SET PIECES:

POWER:

FITNESS:

PACE:

DRIBBLING:

BIRTH PLACE: MOGI DAS CRUZES, BRAZIL

PREVIOUS CLUBS:
SANTOS

INTERNATIONAL:
BRAZIL

NEYMAR
FORWARD

DID YOU KNOW?
Neymar was just 17 years old when he made his professional debut for Santos and just 18 when he played his first match for Brazil.

WHAT THEY SAY...
"The greatest figure of this Brazil team is Neymar. We see that he has no vanity, he is also motivated on the pitch and this motivates his team mates, he always has the intention of winning."
Juninho Paulista, ex-Brazil midfielder

SHOOTING:

BALANCE:

TOTAL: / 110

SKILL:

EXTRA TIME *Neymar rejected the chance to join Barcelona's fierce rivals Real Madrid when he was 15 years old.*

TOP TWEETS

SHOOT MAGAZINE @shootmagazine · · ·

Twitter has become a way of life for millions of people across the globe. And this is no different for the world's top footbellers, with many taking to the social networking site to share their thoughts. Here are some tweets from players praising their fellow professionals.

Vincent Kompany @VincentKompany · · ·

Proud to be amongst great players like @Toure_yaya42 & @hazardeden10 in this year's PFA team of the year! Thx to all!

Like   Retweet   Favourite   More

The Manchester City skipper is delighted to be named alongside team-mate Yaya Toure and fellow countryman Eden Hazard in the 2014 PFA Team of the Year.

Zlatan Ibrahimović @Ibra_official · · ·

Hey @MATUIDIBlaise I saw your goal last night. Magnifique. You must have been watching Zlatan in training. #DareToZlatan

Like   Retweet   Favourite   More

Zlatan Ibrahimovic cheekily hints that Blaise Matuidi's goal for France against the Netherlands came from watching the Swede on the PSG training ground.

Rio Ferdinand @rioferdy5 · · ·

Ryan Giggs retires today....so many gold medals he puts B.A. Baracus to shame! No player adapted their game as well & as effective as Giggsy.

Like   Retweet   Favourite   More

Former Manchester United star Rio Ferdinand pays tribute to team-mate Ryan Giggs after the Welshman announced his retirement.

Joseph Barton @Joey7Barton · · ·

Everton don't look as strong at the back without @sylvaind15tin. Sometimes you only realise how good a player is when he isn't there.

Like   Retweet   Favourite   More

Joey Barton hails former team-mate and current Everton defender Sylvain Distin.

Daniel Sturridge @D_Sturridge · · ·
S/o to the England u17s for winning the European champs. Big things right there!

Like   Retweet   Favourite   More

England striker Daniel Sturridge congratulates the U-17s on winning the Euros.

SUPER SELFIES

Social media has become a major part of football in recent years and with a number of high profile footballers having twitter and instagram accounts, the 'selfie' craze has allowed these players to take supporters behind the scenes.
Here are some of the best examples from the last year...

SAMUEL ETO'O, DAVID LUIZ AND WILLIAN

Following Chelsea's dramatic Champions League quarter-final win against Paris Saint-Germain, the Blues stars appeared in a 'Chelfie'.

DIDIER DROGBA AND WESLEY SNEIJDER

The Galatasaray duo posed for a photo following their win in the Turkish Cup final.

ALEX OXLADE-CHAMBERLAIN, DANIEL STURRIDGE AND JACK WILSHERE

The three England stars posted a picture on the plane on their way to a training camp in Portugal prior to the World Cup.

ALEX OXLADE-CHAMBERLAIN

Following Arsenal's FA Cup win against Hull City which gave them their first trophy in nine years, the young midfielder decided to toast the occasion with a photo of the ecstatic Gunners fans.

JURGEN KLOPP

You don't often see managers getting involved with things like this, but the Borussia Dortmund boss proved to be an exception when he photo bombed a young fan with Marco Reus.

JOLEON LESCOTT, VINCENT KOMPANY AND JOE HART

The Manchester City skipper took this photo following the side's Premier League title win after victory against West Ham United on the final day of the season.

SAM SLOCOMBE

The Scunthorpe goalkeeper had so little to do during his side's 5-1 home win against Portsmouth that he posed for a photo with the travelling supporters.

WOJCIECH SZCZESNY

Following Arsenal's FA Cup win against Hull City and subsequent trophy parade, the goalkeeper decided to get a photo of the Gunners fans who turned out.

WEST HAM

At the Hammers' end of season awards party, striker Andy Carroll managed to snap him and his team-mates looking smart in their suits.

WHERE AM I?

There are so many transfers in modern day football that it's sometimes hard to keep track of which players play for which clubs. Can you help out these confused stars by telling us which team they were playing for in the pictures, and which side they were registered to at the start of the 2014-15 season.

KIT PICTURED:

CLUB AT START OF 2014-15:

KIT PICTURED:

CLUB AT START OF 2014-15:

KIT PICTURED:

CLUB AT START OF 2014-15:

LUKASZ FABIANSKI

MAURO ZARATE

SYLVAIN DISTIN

HEURELHO GOMES

RICKIE LAMBERT

KIT PICTURED:

CLUB AT START OF 2014-15:

KIT PICTURED:

CLUB AT START OF 2014-15:

MATTHEW UPSON

JORDI GOMEZ

FEDERICO MACHEDA

KIT PICTURED:

CLUB AT START OF 2014-15:

KIT PICTURED:

CLUB AT START OF 2014-15:

KIT PICTURED:

CLUB AT START OF 2014-15:

Football rivalries play a massive part in making the sport what it is today. They are the matches fans first look for when the fixtures are released and the games that matter most with bragging rights very much on the line.

On the left are five clubs. All you have to do is match them up with their rivals on the right. This will give you five feisty football rivalries.

Like those crunch matches, this is a game you really don't want to lose. **GOOD LUCK!**

ARSENAL

BLACKBURN

CRYSTAL PALACE

NEWCASTLE UNITED

BURNLEY

BRIGHTON

EVERTON

78

TOTTENHAM HOTSPUR

SUNDERLAND

LIVERPOOL

FUNNY OLD GAME

Sometimes football can get too serious.
So *Shoot* takes a light-hearted look at our favourite game...

"ME!"

WHO WANTS CAKE?

SCORING WAS A LOT EASIER WHEN THE DEFENDERS WERE ASLEEP.

SAM NEEDED A HUG FROM HIS INVISIBLE FRIEND AGAIN...

"HOLD ME"

"NO ONE CAN SEE ME IF I STAY LIKE THIS RIGHT?"

PHIL JONES DIDN'T REALLY WANT TO BE SEEN AFTER THE SEASON UNITED HAD.

"WHAT YOU LOOKIN AT!?"

THE NEWCASTLE FAN WISH HE HAD KEPT THE RECEIPT.

"NOOOOOOOOOOOOOOOOOOOOO!"

ROMAN DIDN"T WANT A HUG.

WHOOSH!

YANNICK BOLASIE GOT BORED OF THE GAME AND DECIDED TO FLY OFF.

"RIBBIT"

FABIANSKI PULLS OUT HIS BEST FROG IMPRESSION AT THE FA CUP FINAL.

SAUREZ HAD BEEN WATCHING TOO MANY KUNG FU FILMS.

POW!

JAY RODRIGUEZ

SOUTHAMPTON AND ENGLAND

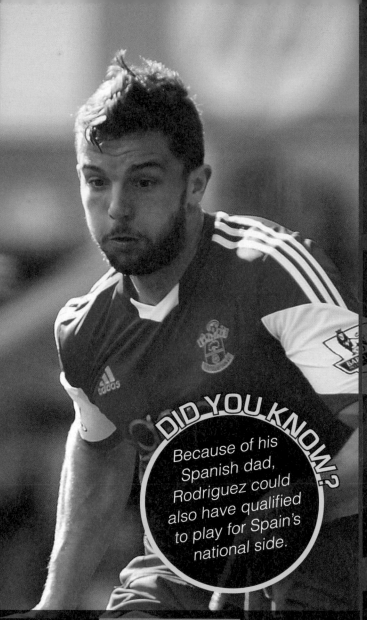

DID YOU KNOW?

Because of his Spanish dad, Rodriguez could also have qualified to play for Spain's national side.

RODRIGUEZ ON...

FIRST ENGLAND CALL-UP

"Words can't describe it. It was a bit surreal. It was a dream come true, really. I couldn't believe it when I was told. Hopefully it will keep improving me as a player."

EX-BOSS MAURICIO POCHETTINO

"Mauricio is a great manager and a great guy and was well-respected by the lads. He worked us really hard and we got good results and finished eighth which we were happy with."

CAREER MILESTONES

December 2007: Made his Burnley debut in the Championship against Bristol City
January 2008: Joined Stirling Albion on loan
March 2008: Scored his first professional goal against Morton
September 2008: Scored his first Burnley goal against Fulham in the League Cup
May 2009: Appeared in Burnley's Championship play-off final win as the Clarets won promotion to the Premier League
January 2010: Joined Barnsley on loan
May 2011: Won Burnley's Player of the Year Award
June 2012: Joined Southampton for £7m
September 2012: Scored his first competitive goals for the club against Sheffield Wednesday in the League Cup
October 2012: Scored his first Premier League goal against Tottenham
November 2013: Won his first England cap in a friendly match against Chile at Wembley
March 2014: Reached 15 goals in a single Premier League season

FACT FILE

Jay Rodriguez
Position: Forward
Birth date: July 29, 1989
Birth place: Burnley, England
Height: 1.85m (6ft 1in)
Clubs: Burnley, Stirling Albion (loan), Barnsley (loan), Southampton
International: England

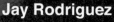

WHAT THEY SAY

"He is a player that is really confident and is playing basically all the games. He has a great dynamism, great technical quality. He is obsessed by football, lives for football, has a great mentality and is always available. The sky is the limit for him. I don't see a roof - there is no limit."

Mauricio Pochettino, ex-Southampton boss.

EXTRA TIME *Despite his impressive goal tally in the 2013-14 season, Rodriguez scored the majority of those from a wide forward position, rather than as an out-and-out striker.*

LEIGHTON BAINES
EVERTON AND ENGLAND

BAINES ON...

EVERTON

"I am very happy at Everton and always have been. It's a fantastic football club and I am excited about what we can achieve here in the next few years. I've loved every minute of being here since I first joined in 2007 and I couldn't be happier."

ROBERTO MARTINEZ

"As a group I think everyone will have learnt a lot from the manager. I have never worked under anyone like him. He is always introducing new things and he has so many ideas about how to play the game."

CAREER MILESTONES

October 2002: Made his Wigan debut against West Bromwich Albion in the League Cup
April 2003: Won promotion to the First Division
December 2004: Scored his first professional goal against Ipswich Town
May 2005: Won promotion to the Premier League as Championship runners-up
August 2005: Made his Premier League debut against Chelsea
February 2006: League Cup runner-up
August 2007: Joined Everton for £6m Made his Premier League debut
March 2009: Scored his first goal for the club against Portsmouth
May 2009: FA Cup runner-up
September 2009: Captained Everton for the first time against AEK Athens
March 2010: Made his full England debut in a friendly against Egypt
May 2011: Won Everton's Player of the Season for the first time
March 2012: Made his 99th consecutive Premier League appearance
September 2012: Scored his first goal for England against Moldova
January 2014: Signed a new four-year contract extension with Everton

FACT FILE

Leighton Baines
Position: Left-back
Birth date: December 11, 1984
Birth place: Kirkby, England
Height: 1.70m (5ft 7in)
Clubs: Wigan Athletic, Everton
International: England

WHAT HIS BOSS SAYS

"I think Leighton is more than a player, he is an icon. He is the best left-back in the country. He is a phenomenal performer and has become a very consistent player for Everton."
Roberto Martinez.

EXTRA TIME *Roberto Martinez believes Baines can emulate Bayern Munich full-back Philipp Lahm and convert to a holding midfielder.*

WHICH BALL?

CAN YOU SPOT WHICH ONE IS THE REAL BALL IN THESE FOUR ACTION PACKED PHOTOS?
WRITE YOUR ANSWERS IN THE SPACES BELOW.

GAME ONE: MAN CITY v SOUTHAMPTON

YOUR ANSWER:

GAME TWO: SPURS v SUNDERLAND

YOUR ANSWER: E

GAME THREE: MAN UNITED v BAYERN

YOUR ANSWER:

GAME FOUR: CHELSEA v PSG

YOUR ANSWER:

MAGICAL MESSI

WE COULDN'T LEAVE WITHOUT HEARING WHAT ARGUABLY THE BEST PLAYER OF ALL TIME HAS TO SAY.....

YOU LEFT HOME AS A YOUNGSTER BUT HOW PROUD ARE YOU TO BE FROM ARGENTINA?

"I've never stopped being Argentine, and I've never wanted to. I feel very proud of being Argentine, even though I left there. I've been clear about this since I was very young, and I never wanted to change. Barcelona is my home because both the club and the people here have given me everything, but I won't stop being Argentine."

HOW PROUD ARE OF ALL YOUR INDIVIDUAL AWARDS?

"I prefer to win titles with the team ahead of individual awards or scoring more goals than anyone else. I'm more worried about being a good person than being the best football player in the world. When all this is over, what are you left with?"

YOU'VE WON EVERYTHING AT CLUB LEVEL AND ARE THE HIGHEST PAID PLAER ON THE PLANET SO WHAT STILL MOTIVATES YOU?

"Money is not a motivating factor. Money doesn't thrill me or make me play better because there are benefits to being wealthy. I'm just happy with a ball at my feet. My motivation comes from playing the game I love. If I wasn't paid to be a professional footballer I would willingly play for nothing."

YOU'VE SCORED OVER 400 CAREER GOALS BUT DO YOU HAVE A FAVOURITE?

"I don't have a favourite goal. I remember important goals more than I do favourite goals, like goals in the Champions League finals, the World Cup or Copa del Rey are the ones that have stayed with me for longer."

ANSWERS

SPOT THE BOSS PAGE 28-29

TRUE OR FALSE PAGE 30-31

1. True
2. False
3. True
4. True
5. False
6. False
7. True
8. False (3)
9. True
10. False
11. True
12. True
13. True
14. False
15. True

QUIZ PART 1 PAGE 32-33

1. Netherlands
2. Sergio Ramos
3. Loftus Road
4. Three (Phil Jagielka, Leighton Baines, Ross Barkley)
5. Burton Albion
6. Argentina
7. Croatia
8. Birmingham City
9. Wigan Athletic
10. Canaries
11. Paolo di Canio
12. League One
13. Belgian
14. Estoril
15. 7 (Coventry City, Newcastle United, Blackburn Rovers, Liverpool, West Ham United, Manchester City, Cardiff City)

WHO AM I?

16. Cristiano Ronaldo
17. Vincent Kompany
18. Kasper Schmeichel
19. Jordan Henderson
20. Charlie Adam

KIT SWAP PAGE 34-35

Gareth Bale: **B,A,D**
Alex Oxlade-Chamberlain: **D,C,B**
Nigel de Jong: **C,B,A**
Zlatan Ibrahimovic: **A,D,C**
Andres Iniesta: **D,A,C**
Mesut Ozil: **A,B,D**
Robert Snodgrass: **B,C,A**
Paul Pogba: **C,D,B**

AROUND THE WORLD
PAGE 38-39

K GARY CAHILL, *ENGLAND*
O EDINSON CAVANI, *URUGUAY*
N DIDIER DROGBA, *IVORY COAST*
I SHINJI KAGAWA, *JAPAN*
J ALAN DZAGOEV, *RUSSIA*
G MILE JEDINAK, *AUSTRALIA*
C CLINT DEMPSEY, *USA*
H NEYMAR, *BRAZIL*
E CHRIS WOOD, *NEW ZEALAND*

HOW DO YOU WANT TO BE REMEMBERED WHEN YOU RETIRE?

"I hope I am remembered for being a decent guy. I like to score goals but I also like to have friends among the people I have played with."

FACT FILE

LIONEL MESSI

Position: Forward
Birth date: June 24, 1987
Birth place: Rosario, Argentina
Height: 1.69m (5ft 7in)
Clubs: Barcelona
International: Argentina

WHAT HIS BOSS SAYS...

"He has won over his team-mates and he has so much talent. The only thing left for him to do is to climb up to the stands, dribble past 10 and then score a goal," *Luis Enrique, Barcelona manager.*

D GERARD PIQUE, *SPAIN*
L ALEX SONG, *CAMEROON*
F MOHAMED SALAH, *EGYPT*
P NURI SAHIN, *TURKEY*
B GIOVANI DOS SANTOS, *MEXICO*
M ROBERT LEWANDOWSKI, *POLAND*
A KARIM BENZEMA, *FRANCE*

GROUND GAME PAGE 42-43

St Mary's, Southampton, 32,589
White Hart Lane, Tottenham Hotspur, 36,284
Camp Nou, Barcelona, 99,354
Bernabeu, Real Madrid, 81,044
Westfalenstadion, Borussia Dortmund, 80,700
Maracana, Flamengo, 78,838
The Valley, Charlton Athletic, 27,111
Elland Road, Leeds United, 39,460
Villa Park, Aston Villa, 42,682
Allianz Arena, Bayern Munich, 71,437

St James' Park, Newcastle United, 52,405
Estádio do Dragão, FC Porto, 52,399
Goodison Park, Everton, 40,157
Stade Velodrome, Marseille, 48,000
San Siro, A.C. Milan, 80,018

PHOTOFIT PAGE 46-47

1: Head-Wayne Rooney. **Eyes**-Jack Wilshere. **Nose**-Gary Cahill. **Mouth**-Steven Gerrard.

2: Head-Samuel Eto'o. **Eyes**-Didier Drogba. **Nose**-Romelu Lukaku. **Mouth**-Daniel Sturridge.

3: Head-Brad Guzan. **Eyes**-Petr Cech. **Nose**-Simon Mignolet. **Mouth**-Hugo Lloris

4: Head-Pep Guardiola. **Eyes**-David Moyes. **Nose**-Diego Simeone. **Mouth**-Roy Hodgson.

SPOT THE DIFFERENCE
PAGE 50-51

NAME THAT YEAR
PAGE 58-59

Barcelona vs Manchester United in the Champions League final - 2011
Bobby Moore lifting the World Cup for England - 1966
'Hand of God' goal - 1986
Manchester City winning their first Premier League title - 2012
Manchester United's treble - 1999
Blackburn Rovers win the Premier League - 1995
Carlos Tevez and Javier Mascherano sign for West Ham – 2006

Wigan win the FA Cup – 2013
Arsenal's unbeaten season – 2004
Nottingham Forest win back-to-back European Cups – 1980

QUIZ PART 2 PAGE 60-61

1. Chelsea	12. Celtic
2. Steve Evans	13. Argentine
3. Japan (Nagoya Grampus)	14. Derby County & Notts Forest
	15. Toronto FC
4. Ashton Gate	**WHAT CLUB AM I?**
5. 49	16. West Ham
6. Martin O'Neill	17.Rangers
7. Italy	18. Portsmouth
8. Ajax	19. AC Milan
9. Allianz Arena	20. Tottenham
10. Ukraine	
11.Middlesbrough	

WHERE AM I? PAGE 68

Lukasz Fabianski
Kit Pictured: Arsenal
Club at start of 2014-15: Swansea
Mauro Zarate
Kit Pictured: Birmingham
Club at start of 2014-15: West Ham
Sylvain Distin
Kit Pictured: Manchester City
Club at start of 2014-15: Everton
Heurelho Gomes
Kit Pictured: Tottenham
Club at start of 2014-15: Watford
Rickie Lambert
Kit Pictured: Bristol Rovers
Club at start of 2014-15: Liverpool
Matthew Upson
Kit Pictured: West Ham
Club at start of 2014-15: Leicester
Jordi Gomez
Kit Pictured: Swansea
Club at start of 2014-15: Sunderland
Federico Macheda
Kit Pictured: Manchester United
Club at start of 2014-15: Cardiff City

RIVALS PAGE 69

Arsenal – Tottenham Hotspur
Crystal Palace – Brighton
Burnley – Blackburn
Everton – Liverpool
Sunderland – Newcastle United

SPOT THE BALL PAGE 74-75

GAME ONE: **B**	GAME TWO: **C**
GAME THREE: **D**	GAME FOUR: **D**